THE LEADERSHIP ACRONYM

11

CORE VALUES THAT MAKES A LEADER GREAT

FOFO THOMAS

BALBOA

PRESS

A DIVISION OF HAY HOUSE

Balboa Press books may be ordered through booksellers or by contacting:

Balboa Press
A Division of Hay House
1663 Liberty Drive
Bloomington, IN 47403
www.balboapress.com
1 (877) 407-4847

ISBN: 978-1-5043-5016-7 (sc)
ISBN: 978-1-5043-5017-4 (e)

Print information available on the last page.

Balboa Press rev. date: 07/13/2016

ACKNOWLEDGEMENTS

I want to show my wholehearted appreciation to the people who have made it possible for me to get this far, without them this book probably would not have been written. I am very grateful to all of you great folks:

John Perez Fafavi (Rev.Dr.)
Harry Bigson
Bright Ladzekpo
Joshua Abbey
Collins Korankye
Michael Paa Kwesi Asare
George Nyame
Jake Kofi-Mensah

PROLOGUE

Though we see leadership all around us and aspire to become a leader. It is surprising everyone's understanding of leadership. We seek to become leaders but neglect to ask ourselves the simple question of *'What is true leadership?'*

We are living in a hypothetical world of power and positional display, and unconsciously many have been blindfolded to conform. So, the reason why many people want to become leaders today is because they want *power;* that is an authority that cannot be challenged, a voice that no one can stand up against–a position full of *"Me, Myself and I"* mindset.

But true leadership is *Influence.* And what is influence? Influence is the *ability* to persuade someone or particularly people to *willingly* do what you want. That means you don't persuade a person by using positional power. You only persuade through reasoning—by allowing the person to either choose to or not to do what you want him to do. Until a person can do something not because he is being coerce, you have not influenced such a person.

The misconception today is that leadership and management are one and the same. But I beg to differ; they are not. There are some differences that distinguish these two.

Leadership *deals with "people"* whereas Management relates to *"things."*

Leaders *lead and work with people*, whereas Managers *manage and control things.* It is in this difference of *'paradigm–responsibility'*—the mental awareness of what a person is liable for—that clearly distinct a manager from a leader. This book is not intended to belittle management but an effort to teach how to apply leadership principles to management roles.

Management

When someone is a manager, his responsibility is to *get things* done. Note I said *"things"* not "people". But ignorantly, some *managing-leaders* (managers who are in leadership positions) see people as things, therefore treat them as such. What they've not realized is, we cannot replace things with people but we can substitute people for things.

Human beings are the creators and designers of things. Things never made man; it's man who invents them. Therefore the substitution of *people* for *things* is the greatest mistake many managers in leadership positions make.

Management is functional (activity oriented), that is why the responsibility of a manager is to get *"things"* done. And mistakenly many liken people with things because the dilemma today is that people are supposed to be *managed*—meaning people need to be controlled, that is why you can see a manager who is successful at getting tasks done but has a poor marital life, feeble relationships, and poor people skills. Management cannot substitute neither can it represent leadership but leadership can invariably stand in the mode of management.

Personal freedom and effectiveness does not emanate from management, it comes through leadership. *Life, as many misconstrue is led, not managed.* We don't manage life, we lead life.

Leadership

True leaders understand that their responsibility is not *only* to get *things* done but to also build and establish true relationships with people. True leaders are not activity oriented; they are people-focused—meaning they don't place activity before people. They take care of their people, while their people take care of their responsibilities. Theodore Roosevelt said, "People don't care how much you know until they know how much you cares."

True leaders are those who take *complex issues*, break it down into the simplest form so a common view is shared. They seek first to understand, then to be understood. They don't focus on position, power or control; rather they establish common grounds that meet expectations in other to get expected work done. Above all, true leaders learn to connect with people so they can effectively work and win together.

About the book

In this book, you will discover leadership qualities a person can cultivate in order to become an effective leader—*a leader that others will love to follow.* Leadership has nothing to do with comfort, rights and belongings.

> Comfort—a place of settlement
> Rights—*power and position*
> Belongings—*a personal place for attaining wealth*

Leadership is influence. Open up your spirit and let's get started.

Contents

PART 1
GETTING STARTED

Chapter: 1

SECURITY

There is so much negative energy in organizations and in our society. People think of taking the legal approach to problem-solving, often at the first blush of problem. Many are looking out for number one, anxious to get their "piece of the pie" and protect their "turf". Such self-centered activity springs from a belief that resources are limited. I call it the scarcity mentality.

— Stephen R. Covey

One of the advantages towards effective leadership is security, probably the first step towards a leader's success. When a leader is not secured, he tends to create barriers between himself and his followers. He competes, because he thinks he cannot succeed as a leader if someone gets first-hand information or knows what he doesn't. He lives in a *self–deceptive* world of limited resources, anxious of being number one. As a result, he neglects his responsibilities in other to compete for personal gains.

He becomes discontent with what he has and where he is because his *scarcity mentality (wrong world view or perspective)* communicates to him, *"life is competitive, be careful no one outshines you or else…you will lose influence."* And because he relies on ego, he tends to fight and do his best in other to protect his turf.

But Stephen R. Covey stated, "Scarcity mentality leaders are people who think life is a finite pie; if someone gets a big piece of the pie, it means less for everybody else. People with a scarcity mentality have a hard time sharing recognition, credit, power or profit. They also have a tough time being genuinely happy for the success of other people…It's almost as if something were being taken from them when someone else receives special recognition."[1]

Leaders and managers who think an employee's ability or knowledge can threaten their leadership position, emotionally become insecure. For they *feel,* if an employee knows what they—the leader— knows and can do what they do then they will lose influence and will not be able to lead.

When a leader embraces this type of mindset, it becomes difficult to share his dreams and goals, for the fear of losing influence and not been able to lead.

But there are leaders with a different kind of mindset, called the *"abundance mentality."* These types of leaders are not intimidated by the capability of their people—an employee or follower's competence does not intimidate them, as a result, they don't threaten people with power. They are able to extend their influence through relationship, mentoring and the development of people.

Insecure Leader

It is very difficult for a leader who is not secure to make other people around him safe. Why? Because you cannot give what you do not *"psychologically"* have. A leader who is not mentally stable cannot make others around him feel safe, a leader who is not bold will

A secure leader is a person who has power over personal influence, but chooses to use himself (as an influence) to get his responsibilities done

not *sincerely* encourage, and a leader who does not trust himself will not offer to trust anyone. It takes the true nature of any leader to have influence. It is the primary reason why leadership has nothing to do with titles, position or power.

Sense of Knowledge

Sam Cawthorn asserted, "The happiest people don't necessarily have the best of everything but they make the best of everything."[2] When I talked about leadership security, I am not referring to money. Yes, a leader can be financially safe and there is no detriment to that. But leadership security refers to the *mental consciousness* of a leader. Because when a leader is unaware of who he is and what is required of him, he neglects his responsibilities in other to fight for personal interest.

I have seen leaders and managers who fight people for recognition. They always insist, "I am the leader (here)," "You do as I say (or...)." But followers are not blind; they know who has the leadership role, even if they don't buy into that person's leadership. So there is no need for a leader to relentlessly remind or threaten people for positional recognition, that's the preserve of insecure leaders.

Leadership security is a sense of recognition; that is, knowing who you are—as a leader—and what is expected of you—your responsibilities. It is not a place that longevity or tradition has rewarded you with or a position you fought others for and is willing to keep.

When a leader thinks he worked his way to attain his current height (that is his leadership position), he will do anything possible in other to protect his position so he can remain in power. But when you understand leadership as influence—the ability to persuade—you will tend to make a difference as a leader.

Isn't it true that when we make sacrifices for something, our tendency is to think we own it? Apparently, that is not true to leadership. A leader, no matter the price he paid or the distresses he went through to become a leader, still needs to discover leadership. That's why Max DePree stated, "The first responsibility of a leader is to define reality."

Every organization rises or falls on leadership. That is why you need to understand that as a leader, you hold the *keys* to your organization's breakthrough. Therefore your *leadership-act* or attitude will determine whether your organization rises or falls.

Insecurity

One of the evidences of insecure leaders is that they don't empower others. They think when they enable people they will become better than they are. So, although they work with people, they have no trust in them, they don't encourage, they don't train, they don't develop and they don't build relationships. Their main concern is to protect their turf and to protect their interests—thus leaving them to selfishness.

Becoming Secure

Many people never understood the essence of being a leader before becoming one. They think leadership revolves around positions, titles and commands, so they aim at it and as they become, they place themselves before responsibility, thereby abusing the authority vested in them.

To become a secured leader, you must:

1. Know where or who you are

Leadership is a responsibility minded but misconceptions have made it seem self-centered and positional. As a result, many think to be a leader is to have dominion. Trying to control, by asking people they come into contact with, "Do you know who I am?" and reminding followers of the damages they can do. But leadership as I have closely observed is *influence*—it is the ability to persuade someone or others so they can *willingly* do what you ask—it goes beyond power and positional display.

Demanding people to recognize your leadership position and the power you have is a form of insecurity and it springs from ego. A secured leader knows;

1. Who he is—*A person,*
2. Where he is—*In leadership,*
3. What he has—*Power over Choice,*
4. And that which is required of him—*Responsibilities.*

To define a secure leader; it is *a person who has positional power over personal influence, but chooses to use himself—as an influence—to get his responsibilities done.* For a leader who does not focus on his responsibilities tends to compete, fight and assault others.

As a leader, if your people are revolting against you, it may not be necessarily because they want power—it's probably because your *leadership-act* or attitude is upsetting them. And if you realize your people are murmuring at your leadership, it's a sign you're not exhibiting true leadership. But there is a good news, you are presently the leader and it will be very influential to take a different approach in order to win their hearts and to become the kind of a leader they will love to follow. John Maxwell clearly puts it, "People don't quit company; they quit the leader."

2. Understand what you have

Leadership is centered on a person. It has nothing to do with titles, positions or powers. When a leader gets to know, "I am a catalyst", he sees, thinks and acts differently. But when a leader sees his value in titles, he turns to rely on it—thereby using it to gain influence and to get things done.

You need to realize as a leader, you have a position, the position does not have you. As a result, you can get things done without the use of power, position or title. And until you get to the point in your leadership, whereby work can be effectively done without you—*the leader*— using or exercising power on people, it's very hard to say you are leading.

Don't place your value on title—by thinking who you are is the position you occupy, rather think differently; knowing that who you are is *where* you are (in leadership), and where you are is *what* you have (personal influence as a tool for getting things done) and what you have is what you use. And *how* you use what you have will determine the type of leader you are. For position and power only takes the nature of him who possess it.

3. Know what you are dealing with

Abraham Lincoln observed, "Nearly all men can stand adversity but if you want to test a man's character, give him power."[4] Leadership can either be a blessing or a curse, depending on the one charting the course. Most people in leadership think their position is superior to them. They think a leadership position is a place of exhibiting power. They tend to cloth themselves with their leadership position and do everything underneath authority. They assign work through commands and control people with power.

When a leader thinks his leadership position is superior to him, then he tends to find comfort in it. But as a leader, you need to understand you make the position, the position does not make you. Power is very deceptive; it can alter your personality. If you don't think so, ask presidents or former leaders. It helps bring everything under your disposal, and if you don't know how to deploy it, it will debase your character, lower your leadership competence and ruin your reputation.

Effective leadership is not in the use of power and position to get things done, to gain influence or to demand respect. Effective leadership is influence; the ability to persuade.

Defining Reality

Insecurity is what draws a line between managers, leaders and employees. Leaders who think a follower's competence can be detrimental to their position tend to abuse power in other to lead.

Knowing who you are and what you are liable for is the foundation to which any leadership value is built. Your first responsibility as a leader is to define reality. By asking yourself the WHY questions:

"Why am I here?" —*realistic question*
"Why am I a leader?" —*responsibility question*
"Why do I want to remain in leadership?" —paradigm question

Is it because you want to make money, to live luxuriously, to prove a point or to lead a particular course or to serve others?

As a leader you must know…

– Where or who you are (as a leader or in a leadership position),
– What you have (yourself as a tool for persuasion)
– And what is required of you (responsibilities)

If you cannot get out of your narcissism so you can empower people, then your insecurity will weaken your leadership. For an organization or a leader who keeps people in boxes cannot experience a major breakthrough.

To ponder

1. Where is my sense of leadership security emanating from?
2. What type of influence do I have on people?
3. Do I know where or who I am, do I understand what I have and do I know what I am dealing with?

CHAPTER: 2

HANDLING OFFENSES

Whenever anyone has offended me, I try to raise my soul so high that the offense cannot reach me.

— René Discartes

Throughout my research, I have discovered that one of the greatest pitfalls of emerging and respected leaders is this; *how they handle offenses*. Each one of us has been offended one way or the other. Offenses are not what we seek out for but it finds its way in our life. And without proper management rob us of self, conscience and sense of joy.

Most leaders think leadership is a 'freeway'—a position full of sweet honey. They don't think of dishonest behaviors because naively they *presume* it never exists there. Then before long, the behaviors they thought never exist, emerges—hitting hard at them. As a result, they lock themselves up in unforgiveness—trying to pay back hurt.

Many leaders are not raising their leadership lid because they have allowed certain offenses to hold them back. Their *leadership-act or attitude* is premised on those wrongdoings. But to lead effectively as a leader, offenses need to be handled.

Offenses

Basically, there are two types of offenses that revolve around every man. The first is *the personal or societal offense* and the second is *the leadership or dependable offense*. In life no one can escape these two. All of us (whether leader, manager, employee, servant or follower) is faced with the personal or societal offense. But leaders are faced with both and the one that detract them (most) is the one pertaining to their job description—the leadership or dependable offense.

There is a mystery many people seemed not to understand and may probably not. I often hear leaders say, "I have tried very hard in this position not to offend anyone—that is the people they lead." And by the time they realize someone has committed a crime against them. As a result, they live their lives backwards—wanting to payback hurts.

You see, we are not living in a perfect world with perfect people; whereby you should be expecting perfection from everyone else. We hurt people and people hurt us.

1. Personal or Societal offense

Personal or societal offenses are those acts of wrongdoings our parents, family members, spouses, children, friends and society commit against us. They are those acts of misconducts which destroy relationships.

As I was writing this chapter, I took time to ask few people the reason why they live in anger, bitterness, frustration and fear. And almost all answers are culpable to someone else. To label a few, many are still angry because of a pass memory—how their parents treated them as a child. Some, how their spouse left them for another, others the way a teacher behaved towards them at school, or the way their community looked down on them, or how they have been duped by a business partner. While majority assert that the *leadership-act or attitude* of their bosses doesn't make them feel comfortable at work.

> If a small thing has the power to make you angry, does that not indicate something about your size?
> —Sydney J. Harris

Each of these persons has someone to blame for their *emotional hurts*. And surprisingly some are looking for an opportunity not to overcome but to pay back. For example some said they don't trust people because they were never trusted or someone abused their trust. Others want to work hard so they can prove a point to those who think they will add up to nothing. Unfortunately, eighty percent of these people I interviewed are leaders of a department, while others are entrepreneurs of a small firm who are not able to lead effectively because they have allowed a past or a present pain to determine the course of their *leadership-acts*. But Sydney J. Harris observed, "If a small thing has the power to make you angry, does that not indicate something about your size?"

I have observed that only few leaders are able to conquer their emotional hurts and move on, majority live with it. And if you can't deal with whatever offense(s) you have in your life, you will end up leading poorly, destroying your reputation and hurting innocent people at the end with your emotional instability.

I've met managers who go to the extent of injuring employees by treating them the same negative way they were treated, either as children, followers or employees. As a result, they cannot effectively relate. If you take your resentments into leadership, you will consciously or unconsciously infect those around you with your 'undealt' pains, anger and frustration.

I have met other leaders who cannot also work effectively with the opposite sex just because of a past experience. Some don't trust people because someone betrayed their trust. When you take your past detriments into leadership, everything that has life begins to die around you because of the negative effect you have on it.

2. Dependable or Leadership offense

The dependable or leadership offenses are those acts of misconducts the people we are leading or empowering affront us with. Every leader faces this challenge and it's the most agonizing battle for leaders. To reflect on;

How will you deal with employees who rise up against you with the least opportunity they get? Or how will you deal with followers who are unfaithful in spite of all your sacrifices for them?

You see, the question is not whether "am I going to be offended?" or "who is going to hurt me?" but "how can I deal with employees or followers who do?" And your attitude towards such acts or behaviors will determine how secured and successful you are as a leader.

Leadership is not a place of certainty, therefore you will face some resistance—not everyone will like, accept, agree or go along with you just because you are the boss. So you will have to learn to deal with followers who don't trust anyone (even you) because someone took advantage of their reliance or followers who don't easily accept correction in other to learn valuable lessons. Or probably, people whom you've lifted up, rising up against you. These are challenges you will face as a leader.

Making a difference

In handling offenses, you must allow the past to influence the present and to let the present impact the future positively. You have to learn to handle offenses with an attitude of forgiving those who hurt you. Because when a leader's heart and mind are in pain, his deeds corrupt moral and his language debase morale.

Forgiveness

Forgiveness is not an easy act to exercise but it's very necessary for a leaders' heart, mind and language to be at peace—in forgiveness. Pastor Andy Yawson of KICC Ghana commented, "Forgiveness is not a feeling but a choice."[2] A leader is not to wait for so-called "right time" to feel to forgive before he or she does so. You must willingly reveal such attitude.

To forgive, you must embrace two things—For and Give.

For—*accept it happened.* There are leaders who have not yet woken up to the past. Their past seems like a nightmare. They live in wonder. They just cannot believe such acts of wrongdoings really occurred to them. They live in a world full of hatred, disliking the people who have wronged them. As a result, their focus migrates from responsibility to revenge.

When a leader doesn't admit the past in order to move on, the past keeps him back. Yes, you have been hurt, taken advantage of and cheated. Admit it, so you can release your heart from *"limitational-hurts" (pains that unknowingly sidetrack and stagnate you).*

When a leader delivers himself from limitational hurts of who did what (to him) and how (it was done), his paradigm (perspectives or world-view) changes. He sees differently and acts differently. He is able to focus on the present—by concentrating on how to take charge of his *leadership-act or attitude* so he can make a difference.

When it comes to handling offenses the past is what shapes your personality *(what you've become)*. And until you learn to deal with offenses, you will unknowingly infect yourself and the people around you because of your emotional instability. As Radiant Impact Revival Commission pastor and leader, John Perez Fafavi commented, "When you hold someone negatively in your heart, you restrain yourself of growth."[3] When you refuse to acknowledge you have been offended in other to release your heart from pain, you will limit your leadership competence and become a nuisance to the people you lead.

> When a leader refuses to let go of his hurts, he denies his leadership progress

Give-*not to repeat.* This act is what doesn't naturally occur in the lives of many people; to let go of an endured pain. Whatever was done to them they do so to others. For example, if someone hurt them they give back hurt, if they were cheated on they cheat on others, if they were mistrusted they also show distrust. Whatever they receive, they reciprocate in other to feel relief.

As I look back to my ten years of working with leaders and managers, I have observed this negative attitude. The first leader I worked with is a given *(repeated)* leader, the second is an effective leader, the third and the forth were also repeated leaders. They made working under them very difficult. I experienced the demonstrations of receiving paybacks of hurts. They treated me so badly as if I was the one who offended them. These are people who laugh with you and the next minute, assaulting you. Their *leadership-act* is premised on an emotionally endured pain they have refused to let go.

You must not pass on the same negative occurrences in your life. Be ready and willing to make the lives of others around you better than you had it. If someone behaved badly towards you, be willing to treat others well in return. If you were treated well, treat others better and if you were treated better, give out your best. By giving out better than you receive, it releases

> When a leader doesn't admit the past in other to move on, the past keeps him back

your heart from pain and the acts of forgiveness begin to take place. Mother Teresa said, "Let no one ever come to you without leaving better and happier." We go to a higher level when we treat others better than they treat us.[4]

Giving Out Better Than You Receive

Every effective leader learns to embrace truth. Feelings are good but they don't help much when it comes to leadership. To be a true leader, you must learn to trust and love people—followers or employees—who don't trust and love as well. Speak for those who speak against you and make sure you are in a true relationship with everyone.

By giving out better than you receive, it helps build a foundation of forgiveness. Just because you are the boss doesn't mean you will gain trust effortlessly. Why? Because trust is a risk people take to have faith in a leader—and if they must take it, it must be worth their emotional sacrifice.

Leadership Baggage

In handling offenses, you must avoid comparison. When you use someone's shortcomings to judge another (as if all are the same), you limit what people can do. But when you acknowledge the past and decide to treat others in a different way, principles come alive while mistakes turn into experience.

> Trust is a risk people take to have faith in a leader and if they must take it, it must be worth their emotional sacrifice.

Yes you have been offended, cheated and taken advantage of and it sounds humanly right to payback those hurts—but as a leader, a person that others depend on, you cannot afford to see every one as a harmful agent or treat people the same negative way you were behaved towards. You just have to let go of such hurts. Jim Rohn stated, "It is not what happens to us, it is what we choose to do about what happens that makes the difference in how our lives turn out."

Forgiveness is not a feeling; it is an everyday exhibited attitude. Civil Rights Movement Leader Martin Luther King, Jr. affirmed, "Forgiveness is not an occasional act; it is a permanent attitude."

When a leader keeps other people's offenses to heart, his leadership comes to a standstill. The reason is because effective leadership involves the use of a pure heart, clean mind and good acts. You cannot afford to poison your heart and mind because of an offense committed against you.

When a leader is not at peace with himself, his thinking becomes fuzzy, and his *leadership-act or attitude* becomes destructive.

When you don't get off your past-offenses, you cannot set good examples and note; if you don't model the right behavior that can be followed, then your life and leadership will impact no one positively.

To ponder

1. Have I been offended?
2. How am I dealing with offenses?
3. Am I ready to let go of those offenses in other to effectively lead?

C H A P T E R : 3

INTEREST

When a leader develops interest in leadership, it moves from self to progress.

One of the best miracles that can happen to a person is when he is in the circle of his influence; knowing that where he is, is of his own will—it is a choice he deliberately made, not a decision made on his behalf. To ask a question; how would you think and act if you are told you will be held accountable for everything that involves you? Will you allow decisions to be made for consequence you are oblivious of, or the ones that you can boldly take responsibility for? You see, when we know we are been watched, we pretend to get the right things done but when we know we aren't, we do things carelessly.

When you know you will be held accountable for whatever work is delegated to you, you become responsible, isn't it? However, when it comes to leadership, many leaders think because they are the head they need no accountability.

I have discovered that, people who *follow or inherit* leadership don't get to become effective. When a person is in leadership because he *wants* to, he gives up (himself—self-interests) so he can gain focus as a leader. But when a person is in leadership because he *has* to, he builds-up (defensive walls) so he can protect his position.

> Whatever make a person a leader is what his values will be founded upon

Leadership as a Choice

Leadership is a choice, a decision you and you alone have to make. How many of us become great or enjoy doing things that are not important—chosen by us? When we get into leadership without a cause or reason, we always have someone or something to blame when we are not able to effectively lead.

But when we are in leadership because we choose to, we ask and search for common answers that will aid us to effectively lead because intuitively we come to understand that our leadership holds the key to the success or failure of the organization.

Leaders who become effective decides to; it is a choice they made and a decision they took full responsibility for.

Making a choice

Today there are many baton (handover) leaders—people who inherited leadership. They did not choose to become leaders; It was bestowed upon them.

One example of an inherited leadership is a family organization that doesn't allow anyone to become the CEO except a descendant. Or an organization that only elevates people because of custom, tradition and longevity. As a result, people become leaders because *they have to*, not because *they want to.*

When we are forced or entitled to become leaders, we tend to rely on our ego, thinking we were chosen because of our high education, smartness, intelligence or how bold we are. And any leader who thinks he is assigned because of these, allows his self–assertions to determine the course of his leadership.

When you are in leadership because you value it, your whole paradigm changes, you see differently, and act differently.

If I have the opportunity to ask you this question;

What made you a leader? And why do you want to lead:
—Is it because you want to make money,
—Live a more comfortable life than others,
—To control people,
—To become famous,
—Or you are a leader because there is a need for leadership, and you
love to lead because you want to add value to people?

Whatever made you a leader is what your values will be founded on. If it is because of money, you will be pursuing money. If it's because of power, position and control then you will be living in ego, looking for popularity and fame—which leads towards bad leadership. But if it's because of helping solve a problem and for serving others then your gifts, talents, abilities, energy and focus will be directed towards making a difference. Whatever your leadership foundations are will determine the values you build on it and the legacy you leave in the minds and hearts of people. It's a conscious and unconscious decision every leader makes.

Leadership Choice

One of the reasons why many leaders don't become effective is because they either fought their way through leadership or inherited it; meaning they did not choose to become leaders. It was either passed on to them or they knocked others down to get there. But you and I can attest to the fact that we only become better at doing things we liberally choose and love to do. Not the one longevity, tradition or heritage rewards us with.

True leadership is a choice. And the word choice comes from *intent*—the mental ability to distinguish purpose from self.

Intent

Intent refers to the *"reason why"* a person wants to be a leader or the *"reason why"* he is in leadership. It is this motive or mission statement that gives and communicates purpose to a leader. It is what will drive your leadership and it acts towards a desired goal. Without intent it will be very difficult for any leader to stay in the circle of his Influence—*knowing who he is, what is required of him and where he is driving his team and organization to?*

Until you develop interest in leadership, you will not be able to invest in it. American author, Henry David Thoreau asserted, "There is no…happiness in any place except what you bring to it yourself."[1] A person who doesn't *choose* to become a leader will tend to become competitive and positional minded, thus leading poorly.

To ponder

1. Did you choose to be a leader or it was imposed on you?
2. From a scale of 1 to 10, with ten been choice, what distractions have you eliminated in other to embrace true leadership?
3. Why do you want to remain in leadership?

CHAPTER: 4

PLAN

A goal without a plan is just a wish

— Antoine de Saint-Exupére

People who get to their desired destinations are those who know where they are going. When someone is leaving a consistent life, it means he planned it. Just picture a man who decides to travel but doesn't know how many miles he has to cover, the volume of fuel needed and the energy to continue but all he is hoping for is to get to that destination. Or a man who wants to start a business but has not first sat down to consider the cost—the capital needed, the place to operate, how long he wants or can stay in business—but his concern is only in making profit. Or let's take a look at a wife who decides to have a child but has not taken into consideration the trauma through pregnancy, child bearing, after birth resources, responsibilities and the child's development. Or for example, two people who want to get married but have not taken time to look at what constitute a wedding; how much they will like to spend and life after marriage but all they are excited about is getting married. Although we don't plan to fail, our failure to plan breaks us down.

Observations

Successful managers and leaders don't just become successful, they chart its course. There cannot be an effective plan without a deliberation and there cannot be a deliberation

Although we don't plan to fail, our failure to plan breaks us down.

when there is no course—the two goes together. Leaders who don't decide to become effective are those who rarely become great. It is possible you can get to a destination without having a plan but you will not get there purposefully.

Every person has an aim and before that aim can be attained *desirably*, it must follow a path. No leader becomes effective just because he has assumed leadership position. When you thrust or force your way into leadership, I can guarantee you four things: you will become tired, frustrated, angry and protective of your position. But when you get into leadership prepared—by defining realism *(why am I a leader)*—you feel secured, learn to work with people as well as develop interest in leadership.

Activity Is Not Accomplishment

Many managers I have observed don't become effective as leaders because they have no leadership course or have not decided on the type of leaders they want to become.

Activity as I have been acquainted with is not accomplishment. The fact that you are getting things done doesn't necessarily mean you are exhibiting true leadership, because there are two ways you can make a person to get a work done; either through coercion or persuasion. If people only do something because they are forced to, not because they want to, you haven't really succeeded as a leader. Truly effective leaders know how to trigger internal motivation for commitment that has people wanting to carry out objectives without…fear of threat.[1]

Plan

Leaders who intend to become effective are those who work towards what they set before themselves. Effectiveness is not a wish; it's the outcome of preparation. Entrepreneur, author and motivational speaker Jim Rohn stated, "If you don't design your own life plan, chances are you'll fall into someone else's plan."[2]

Many of the leaders as I have searched out are going nowhere because their leadership lacks a course. They are only following tradition and doing what's current. What they see other leaders do is what they urgently imitate. They have no vision—they stand for nothing and as a result are dying for anything.

No one successfully gets to a desired destination without having a course. In the power of visionary leaders, Myles Munroe commented, "Leadership without a destination is activity without a meaning". Therefore effective leadership is a course for preparation, and those who decide to become great leaders, become by defining their course.

To decide to be a great leader, you must…

1. Want to be a leader

Leadership is a cause of preparation towards a particular course. To choose or want to be a leader is good but that's not all there is to leadership. To become an effective leader is to decide on *what* type of leader you want to become—whether *Positional, General* or *tradition, Specific* or *Generational leader.*

– A *Positional leader* is a leader who uses *only* power to get things done. These types of leaders don't care about the incentives of other people. All they are concerned about is self, power and success. And because they love to hold power they will do everything possible to maintain position and to protect their interests.

– A *General or the traditional leader* is a leader who follows a particular trend of leadership. He searches out for what other leaders do so he can practice them as a leader; he is not ready to learn anything new than what's current—what others leaders are doing. These types of leaders are afraid of risk, they will rather not try to do something new than to try and fail.

– *Specific leaders are leaders* who are leading but want to take their leadership to a whole new level by learning to apply valuable lessons. These are leaders who do different things. They are not afraid of taking risk or in making mistakes—learning to improve is their language. They are the type of leader's coach John Wooden pointed out, "If you're not making mistakes, then you're not doing anything…a doer makes mistakes."

– *Generational leaders* are leaders who deal with visions and dreams. They rarely occupy themselves with goals; they live for the current generation and think generationally. They are always looking for what they can do that will add value to others—even for the unseen generation. They act selflessly and are not self-centered. They are leaders who believe in self-sacrifice. Their attitude describes what writer Melissa de la Cruz said, "Love meant…sacrifice and selflessness. It did not mean…happy ending, but the knowledge that another's well-being is more important than one's own."

Every leader belongs in these four categories. Those who decide to become effective leaders belong to the last two group and those who have no plan or course for leadership are associated to the first two. Which group do you find yourself in? To decide to become a leader is to realize the *need* for leadership.

2. Agree with leadership principles

Principles are the same; they don't change. They are not facts neither are they personal beliefs but laws; the guidelines of any pursuit. Successful leaders are not people who violate principles for a personal right or wrong reasons. They rather search out for and make unknown ones applicable to their life and mission. If you desire to become a great leader, learn to embrace leadership principles.

3. Love to be a leader

Whatever we love, we embrace—Isn't it? When you develop interest in leadership, its journey becomes enjoyable. Leadership itself is not lonely as many assert, leadership is about connecting—building relationships. Leadership becomes lonely when a leader separates himself from others or wants to feel important. If you desire to be an effective leader, learn to connect with people.

4. Learn from people

It is either ignorance or arrogance that makes people to expect a different result from doing the same thing over and over again. It's said, the day you stop learning you start dying or as Rick Warren clearly put it, "The moment you stop learning, you stop leading". Effectiveness doesn't emanate from activity, it comes through applying right principles.

As a leader, you must learn to cultivate a right attitude—a teachable spirit—in other to effectively lead. Don't be a leader who cannot be taught because he thinks he has all answers. Journalist and author Hunter S. Thompson stated, "No man (is) so foolish but he may sometimes give another counsel, and no man (is) so wise that he may not easily err if he takes no counsel than his own. He that is taught only by himself has a fool for a master."

A teachable spirit is a mindset that does not think it knows it all; an attitude that is not boastful, a mind that is ready to listen, to learn, to unlearn and to relearn. When a leader develops a teachable spirit, he becomes secured, learns to know what he doesn't know, knows more about what he already know, and learns to embrace truth.

To test your teachability, leadership expert John Maxwell recommend, you ask yourself this questions.

1. Am I open to other people's ideas?
2. Do I listen more than I talk?
3. Am I open to changing my opinion based on new information?
4. Do I readily admit when I am wrong?
5. Do I observe before acting on a situation?
6. Do I ask questions?
7. Am I willing to ask a question that will expose my ignorance?
8. Am I open to doing things in a way I haven't done before?
9. Am I willing to ask for directions?
10. Do I act defensive when criticized, or do I listen openly for truth?

If you answered no to one or more of these questions, then you have room to grow in the area of teachability. You need to soften your attitude, learn humility, and remember the words of John Wooden: "Everything we know we learned from someone else! [5]

> It is ignorance that makes people expect a different result from doing the same thing over and over again

5. Live like a leader

Every traveler knows the detriment of his journey. He is aware; 'if I continue the journey moves on, if I stop the journey comes to a halt.' He understands 'I make the journey.'

As a leader, you have to understand, you (as a person) make leadership, not your title or position. If you cannot function without exhibiting power then you are not leading. Your position must depict who you truly are, not what you can do with it. When you substitute position for character, you learn to lead consciously, as a result, your leadership becomes simple, understood, followed and admired. Mahatma Gandhi affirmed, "A man of character will make himself worthy of any position he is given."

To ponder

1. What course is your leadership on?
2. What type of leader are you?
   —General,
   —Traditional,
   —Specific or
   —Generational

Summary

Successful people don't just become successful, so is it with every leader who becomes effective. In becoming an effective leader, you must first define reality. You must know *why* you want to be a leader and *why* you are a leader—your personal reason (conviction) and the main reason (responsibilities).

When you know why you are a leader, your leadership then follows a course. You then learn to amend wrong views for the right ones.

Effective Leadership

There are two main reasons why majority of leaders don't become effective.

One is because they don't have mission statements—a guiding course—a direction for their leadership. They have no focus; they dissipate their energies and act according to feeling. They don't accept responsibility and they blame others for their failure.

The second greatest reason why leaders fail to lead is because they don't learn to handle offenses (past and present wounds). They allow the wrongdoings of others to dominate and weigh them down. They think they cannot set themselves free unless they react to certain offenses. But to go up, a leader must give up. You cannot hold a man down without staying down with him.

Character in Leadership

Leadership is a character and people business. When you allow your personality *(what you have become)* to precede your character *(who you are)* many things, even integrity is overlooked. Our behavior is a function of our personal encounter and *understanding* of the world while character or attitude springs from the core—*the depth of one's being.* Who we have become is the effect of our personal view or encounter with the world but who we are is the tendency to live as beings. When you hold others down, remember, you unconsciously stay down with them.

Applying the Ship Principle

Learning to apply the "SHIP" principle is a guarantee towards personal and organizational breakthrough. When you learn to apply the "SHIP" principle, not only will you win with people, you will become the kind of leader others will love to follow.

To Apply the 'SHIP' Principles

---

1. Acknowledge that leadership security springs from within—it comes from self, not position.
2. Learn to handle past, present and future offenses.
3. Acknowledge that what becomes important to you is what you place value on. Our priority doesn't begin with things that matter least.
4. Chart a course for your leadership. The direction you go is the path your leadership follows. When you fail to plan, remember you've unconsciously planned to fail.

PART 2
UNDERSTANDING PRINCIPLES AND APPLYING THEM

In this second section we will look at the seeming difference between good and great leadership.

When a leader takes assumptions into leadership, he either underestimates people and their job responsibility or makes things come to a stop. When I get the privilege of talking to managers or leaders, I do advise them not to be playing the *"assumption game."* Thinking employees or followers will understand what have been delegated or must know what is expected of them is a **BIG** mistake managers and leaders make. An employee or a follower in any organization or department will use assumption to get any unclassified work done.

Almost 80 percent of the 986 employees we've interviewed assume their leaders know better. By that they think the leader knows who they are, what they are doing, how to delegate, when to praise and what to reward. And as a leader, you cannot afford to chart that hypothetical course with them. When both leader and employee assume *what is not* as something that is, confusion is what results.

If employees use assumption, which are conjectural to determine their leader, you as a leader cannot use assumption to expect results from them. When you think employees must know while employees also assume you know, work done becomes ineffective.

Defining realism is the foundation towards effective leadership. As a leader, you must learn to grow, lead to be followed, exhibit to win hearts, educate to make and multiply progress, connect to reach common grounds and appreciate to promote uniqueness. Knowing what you are responsible for is what you become responsible to.

CHAPTER: 5

LEARN

"I don't think of a man who is not wiser today than he was yesterday".

— Abraham Lincoln

Today, many people all over the world call themselves leaders. And as a matter of fact, it is very easy for someone to wake up tomorrow and say he is a leader and there cannot be a doubt about that. Why? Because we are all entitled to certain leadership, but what many of us fail to understand is that to be called is not to be. The fact that a person is called a leader doesn't mean he or she is a leader. To be called and to be are two different things.

Each one of us has the capability to become good leaders. But because of pride, arrogance and self-centeredness we don't become the kind of leaders we are destined to be. Majority of the leaders I researched think their leadership has arrived the moment they take office. So they stop personal growth, and neglect responsibility. Their focus becomes self—fighting for personal gains. Competing and comparing themselves with others, thereby losing their sense of education and responsibility.

As a man thinks

Many leaders have now become positional minded all because of their self-involvement—how they see themselves. They *think* they are the good among the bad. Although leadership is self, it is not centered on who you are as a person, but the *influence* you have.

Leadership has become a tradition to many, they don't want to engage themselves to learn. The basic idea they have about leadership becomes their entire leadership principle. They hold on to it *hoping* it will make them effective. They don't commit to learn because they think they know it all.

But I have discovered that although principles remain the same, its application varies. If you take housing for instance, a house is built by laying a foundation. But not all completed houses takes the same form. That's why yesterdays demonstrated leadership practice may not aid you today or tomorrow if you don't learn to build other values around it. Patrick Otieku-Boadu writes, "We cannot run our lives and institutions on old paradigms. What was a solution for yesterday can even pose as problem for today."

> Dictating to people is good, it feels good but it will not mark you as a great leader—sharing power does

It amazes me, the leadership skills most leaders are deploying today were the same skills which were exhibited in the nineteenth and twentieth century. Although these leadership skills function, its impact and response does not satisfy expectations.

Leadership skills which were used fifty or hundred years to achieve great results can still be exhibited today but its impact will not be commensurate to today's challenges and demand. Let me take you to the automobile world. Do you know, the ground breaking idea established in manufacturing a car is still relevant today—getting things and people from one place to another conveniently—but the concept keeps

> Leadership is much self, but a better service

on getting added values? It's not the old idea that makes a difference today in car manufacturing or car purchase, it's the added value.

Why do you think the Ford Model T is not the same cars we are driving today and why are different cars been manufactured? Is it because car manufacturers want to produce more cars, I don't think so. You see, human beings are changing, we are desiring and moving towards different things because of everyday unprecedented and emerging ideas. As a result, people are not looking for 2-speed planetary gear cars neither are we looking for 1909 no door roaster cars.[1]

Cars are manufactured today not necessarily because you and I have some distance to cover or goods to carry, even though that may seem to be the ground breaker. But today cars are manufactured significantly for safety, convenience and satisfaction of the user. We have cars with sophisticated gadgets; like airbags, navigators, CD/DVD players and cars that can travel on 240 km/h to 430km/h compare to the Ford Model T, which travelled 64 to 72 kilometers per hour. Even though the ground breaking idea has not changed, values have been founded on it.

Will you *love* to drive a Ford Model T, if it's offered you today? If not, then I guess you cannot depend on what you know today as your leverage in leadership. You have to keep growing yourself. A farmer cannot continue to use yesterday's way of farming today, if he wants to meet demand, competition and challenges.

Character, Attitude and Personality

Effective leadership is not centered on personality, although personality plays a part, the emphasis is on character and attitude. When we talk about Character, Attitude and Personality...

—Character represents *who* you are,
—Attitude resolve on *what* or *who* you want to become,
—Personality refers to *what* you've become.

It's attitude that invokes character not personality. Leadership has little to do with what we feel, think or see of it. Most leaders place value on their personality than attitude.

Our personality depicts what we've become (from experience and viewpoints), but attitude represents who we are. Our personality is the way we learn to think and feel about a thing whereas attitude is the way we deal with such thoughts and feelings.

Character, personality and attitude are what distinguish winners from losers. Winners are those who know and act while losers are those who know but hope things will work out for them. We cannot substitute personality for character—it is futile to do so.

Attitude exemplifies who you are; it is what gives you a sense of meaning and that which drives you towards a philosophical goal. It is the best reason why feedback is a leader's best friend; because it is the only thing that communicates the true behavior of a leader. Leaders' who don't like receiving feedbacks are those who don't effectively get to grow and to successfully lead.

> When a leader loses his sense of identity and responsibility, he tends to follow and do what he sees, feels and think is right.

Practice and Learning

It is obvious many are now *practicing* leadership instead of learning it. Practice is a very necessary tool in leadership but it must not become the primary cause for your leadership. Majority of the leaders I researched observed their leadership. Their *leadership principle* was observed and practice from their mentors or influencers. Wherein they talk like them, dress like them, eat like them, get angry like they do, laugh and smile like them, meet and address people like they do and even ignorantly live their marital lives like their predecessors. They have practice everything from followership (observation) to their leadership level and cannot let go of such practices. They admire them so much that they have become their leading picture.

True leadership is less about your thoughts and feelings. Leadership is influence—the ability to persuade. Yes, we are supposed to observe some leadership practices but not to imitate personality. Because you cannot be like any other leader—the only person you can best be is yourself. When a leader loses his sense of identity and responsibility, he tends to follow and do what he sees, feels and thinks is right.

To Ponder

If you are a leader, I want you to pause at this point for five to ten minutes and take a critical look at your leadership. And ask; where are my leadership principles and practices emanating from? Because the leadership practices you have are no different from the leader you are.

Reading and Learning

One of the remarkable sayings I hear from people who persuade themselves to learn is, "I've learned and learned but things don't seem to change." To make it clear; there is a difference between reading and learning. And until you understand this truth, no matter the quantum of information you have, your life and leadership will be no different than where it was five or twenty years ago. I have come across leaders (some friends) who have not been transformed by the quality of information they share with people.

Reading is good but it does not produce results. People who read are those who get informed. And information on its own does not produce results. There are many informed leaders who are not successful even though they have all the information's necessary to uplift them. They rather love to share what they know than to apply it. Their interest lies in gathering information and not in how they can allow what they know to make a significant difference in their lives and leadership.

> Education consists of what we have unlearned
> -Mark Train

Reading and learning is one of the characteristics that differentiate school teachers from leaders. Teachers know to teach while leaders learn to lead. Obviously, it is this distinction that makes all the difference. We read to become acquainted with knowledge but learn to get influence by what we know. Stephen R. Covey stated, "To learn and not do is really not to learn. To know and not to do is really not to know." So if what you know as a leader is not having any effect in your life and leadership then I can explicitly say your leadership is only in the information mode—and you must graduate from that class.

Sacrifice

Leadership is not a set achieved target (a destination) but a place of continual growth. Effective leaders are learners. They are not afraid of making mistakes or sacrifices. Mistakes are part of leadership; for it is in mistakes *(miss taken)* that lessons are learnt. Buckminster Fuller stated, "You can never learn less; you can only learn more. The reason why I know so much is because I have made so many mistakes." Leaders who are afraid of making mistakes don't get to learn valuable lessons.

Every information comes out with its own price and leaders who are afraid to pay the price will not enjoy the reward. It is easy to pick up a book and read but very difficult to apply what you've read. Leaders who learn the leadership language are those who take into account what they know. And not only do they reflect on it; they make them applicable. For the only way to learn, unlearn and relearn is to act on what you know. As the common saying goes, *"practice makes perfect."*

Attention

Learning leaders are very attentive. Attention is what distinguishes readers from learners. Readers are very positive and optimistic about what they know whilst learners are very decisive about what they know. Readers read to become acquainted, learners learn to get influence. Learners have a way of connecting what they read and know to their lives and leadership. Because without envisioning or relating what you know to your life and leadership, it will be very difficult to find yourself at fault if you are not demonstrating good leadership.

I have come across leaders who don't realize that their insecurity, narcissism or ego can limit their leadership; rather they think an employee or a follower is responsible for their leadership and organization's failure. So they blame others.

Attentiveness is what effective leaders use as a learning tool and it is what points out to them if a change is needed. If you are not closely examining your leadership with what you know, how then can you identify whether you are leading right or wrong?

The wrong wall

Today, many leaders' leadership concepts are leaning on a wrong wall. And because their leadership is practice, they continue to repeat mistakes without recognizing them. When leadership becomes self instead of what we are liable for, we vent our feelings and thoughts unconsciously.

There are leaders who treat followers the same negative way they were treated by their ignorant influencers. They don't like receiving feedback, they are not interested in learning new things or making attitudinal changes, they love the status quo. Their words mostly ring in my ears, "who are you to correct me?", "how many years have you been in leadership?", "I am the leader here." Their prideful attitudes imprison their spirits of teachability. They think leadership is defined by having followers—so they can claim, "These are my people", "I made them who they are." Thereby demanding to be respected, appreciated, love and be called by a chosen name.

As a leader, you must seek first the interest and the impact you can make in the lives of the people you lead. And when you are able to make a difference in their lives, then they will give you the title. We don't get positional minds before influence, it's vice versa—when you become an influence, title(s) follows.

True Leadership

True leadership is a shift in paradigm—in the way we think, perceive and understand the world. Leadership is not made for a specific group of people but true leadership is required of them occupying such position.

Learning as a Language

The language of leadership is education. In power shift, Alvin Toffler specified, "The illiterate of the 21st century will not be those who cannot read and write but those who cannot learn, unlearn and relearn." Leaders who learn the leadership language are those who commit themselves not only to knowledge but are able to dilute their wrong views for the right ones.

Growth is not an automatic process as John Maxwell established. It takes education. And "Education" as Mark Twain remarked, "Consists of what we have unlearned."[2]

Personality and Ego

Physiologist Claude Bernard pointed out, "It is what we think we know already that often prevents us from learning."[3] Leaders who don't engage themselves in learning are those who don't get the chance of exhibiting true leadership. When a leader is living in ignorance, he depends on position and ego for survival. But effective leadership goes beyond personality (self). True leaders don't become effective because of their self-involvements. It is in the lessening of an ignorance that they are able to climb the leadership ladder of greatness.

When you put yourself (ego) ahead in leadership, you preclude growth, thereby leading egoistically. Cuban author Anaïs Nin remarked, "We don't see things as they are, we see them as we are."[4] If a leader refuses to see things as they are and see them as he is, he begins to rely on position thereby neglecting his responsibilities. But note, placing yourself above your leadership responsibilities are a real deception towards effectiveness.

Admission Of ignorance

One disadvantage I have noticed in the lives of many unsuccessful leaders is, they *"think"* they *know* it all. They don't want to admit the fact that they can go to a higher level just by acknowledging they don't have all the answers.

When a leader thinks he knows it all, he paralyses his leadership ability. And since he doesn't accept reality, he defeats himself.

Leaders, who hold on to their *thoughts and feelings thinking* they cannot be taught, end up limiting their leadership competencies. Every true leader I have met admits, "Am still learning, or I don't know it all." As Basket Ball Coach John Wooden affirmed, "It's what you learn after you know it all that counts."[5]

It is in the realization of *"I don't know it all"* that keeps true leaders seeking for possible answers each day. Leaders who don't admit they don't know it all are those who become *jack of all trades* and *master of nothing*. True leaders don't argue to satisfy their ego on issues they lack knowledge in; they work on their

> Admission of ignorant doesn't mean you don't know who you are, what you are responsibilities for and what your values are, it simply means you are not the source of all knowledge

ignorance. If it's a lesson, they humble themselves and learn, if it's a shortcoming, they accept and work on it. Sydney J. Harris commented, "When you run into someone who is disagreeable to others, you may be sure he is uncomfortable with himself.

When you put your feelings and thoughts behind your responsibilities, you learn to successfully lead. True leaders acknowledge they don't know everything and they don't fight that. Just because you are the boss doesn't mean you are the source of all knowledge.[6] The moment you think *you know it all*, you preclude yourself of growth.

One influential step true leader's take that you can also act on, in other to grow is to admit you don't know it all and you are ready to be taught a learnt lesson. When a leader is always arguing to win a conversation he lacks facts on or becomes too argumentative, he loses the trust and respect of people. Admission of ignorance doesn't mean you don't know who you are or what you are responsibilities for and what your and values are, it simply means you are not the source of all knowledge. And none of us are.

To learn

To learn is to seek out—for something—and hold to it. Your decision to grow should not be left to chance. When you decide to grow, you must embark on a journey, called *research*. The word research is derived from the old French word recerchier, which comes from two compound words "re and cershier or search." [7] Where I will define *RE* as a natural state of a thing, and *SEARCH* as the effect of such thing. So from a leadership point of view, If *Re* is "information", *Search* then focuses on the "effect" of such information.

If a leader decides to learn good communication skills, that decision drives his passion, as it is an ability he wants to master. Meanwhile, the communication *information* he seeks out for is termed as *Re,* and the *effect* of such information is referred to as the *Search*.

Don't invest your time on things that will not aid your quest towards effectiveness. Read on materials that will help you lessen a particular ignorance as a leader. If your attitude or relationship with people doesn't encourage you, buy books, listen to audio's and attend conferences that will open up your spirit on how to embrace positive attitude.

Information should not just be sought for; its outcome must be taken into consideration. The outcome of any information a leader seeks out for is as important as the information itself. You cannot be a doctor whiles acquiring knowledge in radio or television broadcasting. You cannot be a pastor and be reading books on machinery, ‖ True leaders see things differently ‖ neither can you be a mechanical engineer and be wasting time with farm tools. The position you occupy or the change needed is the kind of information you should seek and invest your valuable time on; for you will only become successful at what you give your time, passion, attention and money to.

Information

As important as information is, it doesn't produce results on its own. Many leaders as I know are in the *re* stage of their leadership, acquiring knowledge; without allowing what they know to transformed them. Some of my friends who are in leadership positions are failing in communication because they've not learned to introduce what they know and have read into their leadership in other to prevent boss and subordinate misconceptions so desired work can be achieved.

The fact that you can communicate, doesn't make you a successful communicator. In sales, it is not what you are marketing that matters, it's the effect of what you are selling that counts. If the outcome doesn't produce desired result, you will soon be out of business. In contrast to leadership, acquisition of knowledge is not everything, the effect of such knowledge is what matters the most.

As a result, research should be sought after on correct, exact and accurate information. You cannot afford to chart course with assumptions. The ignorance in many unsuccessful leaders is the arrogance to follow things that doesn't work.

Any information you seek out for must be examine at its effective level. The effect of an information or knowledge is important as the information itself. Don't *assume* information is universal, because it worked in another person's leadership, it will work for you. You must first take a look at your values and examine whether the effect of such information will bring positive and acceptable transformation in your life and leadership.

Secret of Success

I have observed leaders who want to become supernatural beings. They wish they could just purchase knowledge; they don't want to commit themselves to learning. Yet they want to be recognized, appreciated and celebrated as a successful leader.

Knowledge doesn't embrace any man, it emanates from education. And guess what, education is gain through the lessening of ignorance. If you are not ready to educate yourself in other to lessen a particular ignorance then your leadership ability will be limited.

Sacrifice

Nothing is gained without something being given. As I have delved into, true leaders are people who give themselves to *continual learning*. Every day is a lesson for them and every lesson is an opportunity towards growth. They give less time to things like television and other media activities that distract focus. They read at least one book a week, attend seminars and listen to audio books in their area of expertise. They live their lives in growth. If they are not reading, they may be reflecting, if they are not reflecting, they may be thinking, if they are not thinking, they may be strategizing, if they are not strategizing, you may find them playing mental games or exercising for good health. Almost sixty to seventy percent of their daily activities are in line with their purpose. They plan their time and work on their plans.

> Research can be defined as the ability to seek right information in the direction that provides a desired result.

If there is any shared ability among effective leaders, it is *time management*—they don't take it for granted. Your leadership growth and development can be measured by what you most spent your time on.

Characteristics

True leaders *enjoy* learning. It doesn't matter who has the *right* message for them. They learn from children, employees, friends and even strangers. Their heart is always open to new ideas; they are ready to be thought. They carry no pride and arrogance in them.

People full of themselves usually don't have much room left for a life-changing dream. That's why it's so important to get rid of pride; it can keep you from trying new things or asking questions because you are afraid of looking stupid. It makes you want to stay in your comfort zone instead of striving for the end zone. Pride puts your focus on appearance instead of potential. And it prevents you from taking risk—something you must do to discover your dream. If you are a prideful person, it's time to let go of your pride and grab hold of your dream.[8]

A teachable spirit is not boastful, it's meek. It says, "I'm ready to learn and I'm ready to receive—I don't know it all—as a result, we are here to complete each other, not to compete with ourselves."

Lessons are not only learnt from books, elderly or well-respected people, lessons can be taught. And if you develop a teachable spirit, it will amaze you what you can learn, unlearn and relearn. A leader can go anywhere and break barriers, if he embraces teachability.

Developing a Teachable Spirit

To develop a teachable spirit, you need to…

1. *Respect yourself and others*—Respect is the foundational key to influencing self and others. If you don't respect people, you will look down on them and underrate their intelligence.

2. *Acknowledge you don't know it all*—Leaders who think they know it all prevent themselves from asking questions and receiving answers. They are not even willing to listen because they think it's a sign of weakness. Admitting you don't know it all is always the first step towards education and teachability.

3. *Accept the fact that others can complete you*—Greatness comes through humility. Thinking only well-known people can teach you what you need to know, is the worst mistake to make. Knowledge is not given to specific group of people; every man has a certain level of experience that is made to complete another. And when you live a teachable life, it will amaze you what you will learn .

Courage

There is one thing that learning requires and that is courage. Courage is the ability *(will-power)* to do a thing despite fear and uncertainty. It has been acknowledged that courageous people are always winners, even if they fail. Because he that tries and fails is better off than he who does not. Thomas Edison failed 1,000 times inventing the light bulb. And when he was asked, he replied, "I didn't fail 1,000 times. The light bulb is an invention with 1,000 times step."[9]

I have worked for leaders who restrict people from giving them feedbacks because they don't have the guts to accept and make amends.

To become a committed learner, you need to exercise courage—the ability to keep doing what you've set before yourself despite changes in conditions. Sometimes it may sound imprudent to learn something from people you are leading or those who are beneath you. But consider this Chinese proverb, "He who asks a question is a fool for five minutes. He who does not ask a question remains a fool forever." If you can be humble and teachable, growth will become inevitable in your life.

ACTION

Most at times it is the fear of the unknown that shuts people in their comfort zone. Without putting what you've leant into practice, you haven't learnt a thing. Coach Don Shula and Ken Blanchard write, "Learning is defined as a change in behavior. You haven't learned a thing until you can take action and use it."[10]

Learn to put what you know, have read and been taught into practice. Remember, learning is defined as *change*—you haven't learned a thing until you can take action and use it.

APPLYING THE FIRST PRINCIPLE

People who don't grow don't make the effort towards growth and those who don't make sense haven't learned to make one. When you don't educate yourself, you will become uneducated. Because what you know today cannot guarantee you success tomorrow. To climb the leadership ladder of greatness, you must commit yourself to growth.

Steps to take….

1. Acknowledge you don't know it all.
2. Be ready to learn, unlearn and relearn.
3. Know that one person cannot teach you everything.
4. Live an educational life.

Remember; Admission of ignorance is the first step towards education.

CHAPTER: 6

EXAMPLE

"Example is not the main thing in influencing others. It is the only thing"

— *Albert Schweitzer*

One of the finest things we all look out for in any person, product or company is its quality exhibition. When a good investor wants to invest in an organization, his consideration is not on the company's building or its number of employees but rather he looks out for one thing—the credibility of such organization.

True leaders are those who *walk their talk and talk their walk*. They do what they say and say what they do. They don't violate promises—they stand by their words.

Human beings are similar to products. The way you lead yourself will determine how important you are and the value people place on you. For example:

How gravitated are you towards people who are not reliable?
How many times have you willingly bought from companies that are not trustworthy?
Or how whole heartedly do you believed in a system that doesn't work?

I know the answer is obvious, but it depicts how you see and will relate to an organization, a person or a system. Similarly, the way you will not rely on organizations, systems or people who cannot be trustworthy will be equivalent to how others will relate to you and your leadership if they don't find trustworthiness in you.

Leadership as a Gift

Human beings are all sensible irrespective of gender or age. The fact that someone cannot read, think positively, act courageously doesn't mean he has no sense of *knowledge (knowing what's right and what's wrong)*. Most at times leaders and managers miss this intuitively in their dealings with people. They want to treat people the way they see, feel and think of them, forgetting that by so doing values begin to diminish and trust vanishes.

When a company's top priority is premised on money or profit making, it produces anything and loses everything. In the same manner, when a leader's priority is ego, he fights people and abuses power. When a husband or wife's necessity is only what he or she wants, abuse becomes inevitable in that family.

True leaders don't limit people when they can lift them. One innate ability you must be acquainted with is that leadership is meant for all—we are all leaders. The way you depict your leadership will determine the level of confidence those you are leading exercise in you.

Egoistic Leadership

In my ten years of leadership training and research, I have seen leaders who never value anything—not even their current status. They think they are supposed to be higher than where they currently are, so they place their personality *(themselves)* ahead of their character, attitude and responsibilities. They seek for a raise in paycheck, higher positions and play work politics. The least they can do for the people they lead is to compete with them for personal gains. They are the type of leaders who create arguments and don't develop winning strategies. They are not in the position to take no for an answer, their opinions are the best ones that count. You either work with it or *'fire'* yourself is their rule. It even happens in families, governments and organizations whereby husbands or wives, presidents and leaders think their decisions are final. But those negative thoughts destroy reputation. A decision becomes final when it is based on facts or it is in line with correct principles.

> As long as you think the problem is out there that very thought is the problem
> –Stephen R. Covey

Liability Leader

Most leaders don't want to think, others don't even realize their importance. The reason why we have been given the thinking faculty is not to outsmart others but to become better with ourselves. Our thoughts are supposed to control our feelings, desires and emotions—not to fight others. A true leader knows he cannot change people but he can model change for them.

A liability leader is a person who looks out for problems in everything and in anyone. Stephen R. Covey said, "As long as you think the problem is out there that very thought is the problem."[1] In other words, you must frequently evaluate your leadership to observe whether it is limiting or lifting—you, the organization or its people. Leaders, who don't want to admit they can become a problem, become a problem. Never blame others for your leadership failure.

Choice

Leadership is influence, not a call or a demand for recognition. Majority of leaders' leaderships are premised on demand—like a change left on a purchased item—where they begin to demand for it. But when a leader begins to ask for the respect he doesn't have, it drives everyone around him crazy.

Just imagine I come to your shoe shop, where every shoe displayed has a price tag on it and I choose a shoe worth fifty Ghana Cedis. After giving you a fifty cedi note, I enter into an argument with you, demanding for a change. What will you perceive and what will be your reaction towards me?

This exemplifies leaders who only become excited about leadership positions—thinking it's a place of comfort. Where they sit and cross their legs *hoping* things will work out for them. Leadership is a place where decisions are made and followed through. Position cannot guarantee effectiveness. If you consider leadership, you will realize it is not only meant for literates, illiterates also become leaders. And most surprisingly, the illiterates somehow lead better than the literates. Why? Because it is not what you expect from leadership that counts, it is what you bring to it that makes all the difference.

> You don't have to hold a position in order to be a leader
> –Anthony J. D'Angelo

Leaders who invest their gifts, time, money and resources in leadership are those who greatly benefit from it. Galatians made it clear that, *"You cannot reap unless you have first sown."* [2] One of the most painful observations in leadership is; you put in more than what you draw out, but it's worth the return. So, if sacrifice is the result of true leadership, what will position without sacrifice produce? Yes, you've got the picture—nothing. It is the best reason why leadership cannot be left at the positional level; for position cannot replace effectiveness. Anthony J. D'Angelo pointed out, "You don't have to hold a position in order to be a leader." [3] What you need is influence.

Commitment

Probably what employees are hungry for, that leaders are not feeding them with is trust—the ability for a leader to talk his walk and to walk his talk, not respect. In an organization, employees are not looking for how respected a leader is because respect can sometimes be deceptive. Your leadership must be built on trust, not respect. There is a difference between *trust* and *respect* when it comes to *true* leadership. I will elaborate on it later. But to be respected is to be regarded *(to be known)* and to be trusted is to be accepted *(to be connected to)*.

We respect people because of their personality—*who and what they've become*. But trust them because of whom they are—*their ethics or values*. Although most celebrities don't exhibit good moral's we still honor them. Don't we? So it is when a leader is respected.

When a leader is respected, he is given the recognition note. If he is trusted, he is connected to in spirit, mind and body. When people respect you as a leader they only try as much as possible to please you but when they trust you, they stay connected and committed in order to learn from you, help you and the organization. When followers connect with you, their reliability is in your values, not person.

It is possible for a person to respect you without having trust in you. Let me draw your attention to this simple truth: why don't you save your money with friends or family members but rather will put it in a bank? Is it because you reverence the bank than your friends, I don't think so, but because you know the bank can be depended upon anytime you need your money. Some of us trust the banks even better than ourselves.

When it comes to leadership, followers expect good morals from you because you are expected to exhibit it. One amazing truth I have discovered in leadership is that followers will not change unless there is a model for change. And guess who must institute that—the leader. If people are not following what you do but rather what you say then there must be something wrong with your leading. One basic fact you must be acquainted with is; people don't follow you (as a person) they emulate the behavior they see in you.

> People will not change unless there is a model for change

Trust and Respect

Walking through leadership, I have discovered that we get respect and gain trust. We don't mostly work towards respect; people give it to us based on their perception of us. You can *never* force a person to respect you, it is in his will that he shows you respect. And when someone gives you respect, there must be a course commitment or a job well done to keep and hold that respect in high esteem or it will just be a sycophant *one*.

An employee may respect his boss based on age, academics or performance (ability to get things done, how good he communicates) but that same employee will not trust his boss with his life.

A person may respect you and not want to do business with you simply because she has not found trustworthiness in you.

Don't we all give respect to people we have not met before? Don't we give our seats in a bus to people just because they are older than us? But I can guarantee you, the same people you stood for you will not trade things of importance with. So the fact that you are being respected as a leader doesn't mean you are leading.

Let me share with you an example of how we demonstrated respect when we were raising funds for our church building years back. Because it was common, we printed a "church-fund" card. And note what was written on it.

Harvest Fire Ministry "respectfully" invites the company of … (name)……to witness its first year anniversary.

Many of these cards were distributed to people we don't even know. But we respected their support and donations. Haven't you humbly received some invitations with regards that you were not even supposed to be a part of? I'm not saying respect should not be admired but it should not become the quest or leading picture of your leadership. One of the advantages in leadership position is that it already commands respect. But ignorance has made many leaders to still fight for what they already have.

Respect in leadership is common because you have occupied a position which commands respect. So to be respected is to be given an opinion. And note; you cannot force anyone to have a high and positive opinion of you unless there is something you've done that can lift and keep that opinion high up.

Trust

True leaders *never* asked to be trusted, they work on that dependency. Trust is earned, not given. The first change a leader should be expecting when expectations are not met is not from his people but of himself. Because followers don't first change to expect change, they adapt to the leader's ethics and values. Effective leaders know they cannot use power and position to change people. They understand, whatever example a leader sets is what's accepted and followed by his people.

Employees or followers adapt to the standard their leader sets. And the fact that you have influence on people doesn't mean you are exhibiting true leadership. Influence is influence, it cannot either be said as good or bad, its produce is what depicts it. A person with a negative attitude has the same power to influence others as a person with a positive attitude. The difference appears in the results.[4]

So to gain trust, you must be trustworthy—by doing what you say and say what you do. Author Ken Kesey observed, "You don't lead by pointing and telling people some place to go. You lead by going to that place and making a case."

People judge us by what we say and do continually. I have met leaders who because have built credibility in one organization, think it will follow them wherever they go, even if they switch companies. But an acceptance in one firm or department will not guarantee you approval in another. If you say you are credible, evidence is the language of every customer, business associates, employees, followers, children, friends, husband, wife and even a stranger.

I have come across leaders who raise their shoulders wherever they go thinking people will praise them because of a former achievement. But until a person can have a personal relationship with you, he will still hold his doubts of you. Why? Because trust is a risk someone takes to have faith in another. And if people must have it in you, it must be worth their emotional sacrifice.

Leaders who exhibit trust are those who are...

1. **Truthful:** St. Francis of Assisi observed, "It is no use walking anywhere to preach unless our walking is our preaching."[5] Effective leaders are those who do what they say and say what they do. They are not leaders who talk positively and act negatively; such a leader cannot be trusted. Followers don't rely on a leader who agrees and disagrees behind their backs or a leader who doesn't practice what he teaches. True leaders say what they mean and mean what they say. When they make a promise, they keep to it.

   > It is no use walking anywhere to preach unless our walking is our preaching
   > —St Francis of Assisi

   As a leader, you must be honest in your communication and dealings with people. If you cannot keep a promise, avoid making uncommitted ones. But if you make a promise and break it, make amends—sincerely apologize and ask for forgiveness. One basic truth about genuineness is that it cannot be faked; for we can all identify with when someone is actually sorry. Nevertheless I have seen leaders who think apologizing to their people on a failed promise is a sign of weakness; rather not doing so is a form of weakness. When you apologize for a wrong done it squares up the emotional hole of the person you've offended and it encourages him or her to keep faith in you. Being the boss doesn't make you sinless. Not making amends for offenses is a true sign of a leadership weakness.

2. **Respectful:** True leaders respect people. What unsuccessful leaders never seem to understand is that people will respect you as *long* as you keep respecting them. If you don't show respect in your organization, followers will not show respect to each other. If you want your people to respect one another, demonstrate it by respecting them. If you don't show respect, no one will.

Quality EX

Effective leadership is not in the quantity of people a leader has raised but the quality of those he has lifted up. For what is worse than training people and losing them? Unsuccessful leaders think leadership is all about having followers or finding someone to lead. But true leadership goes beyond that. It is the basic reason why not all school teachers become leaders; they only teach, they don't lead.

True leaders understand that acquisition of knowledge is not the heart of effective leadership. The fact that you are knowledgeable doesn't mean you will make a great leader. Laurie Beth Jones affirmed, "Information after all, is a neutral tool. The wisdom to know how to use that information is what is in most demand today." Great leadership is shown when knowledge is coupled together with a positive attitude.

I have worked with leaders who don't seem to understand the reason why those they've helped, have deserted them. They assert;

"Oh, I taught him everything he knows",
"I was his mentor"
"I brought him this far",
"If it wasn't for me…"
"Now that he has become….he has forgotten where he came from, ungrateful person."

One of the reasons why followers become ungrateful to their leaders is when they *(the leader)* were unfaithful to them under their leadership. The way you treat people when they are beneath you will determine the way they deal or behave towards you. Whitley David pointed out, "A good supervisor is a catalyst, not a drill sergeant. He creates an atmosphere where intelligent people are willing to follow him. He doesn't command; he convinces."[6]

Example in General

True leaders are those who leave positive marks in the minds and hearts of people wherever they are. People easily imitate what they see quicker than what they hear. Consider these adages, "Seeing is believing", or "Action speaks louder than words." When a leader is narcissistic (full of himself)—thinking he must be seen, known, appreciated and loved, he misses the leadership mark.

Whether people know you as a leader or not, they still want to be certain you can be relied on. Followers are not astounded about who you are because in their minds they've already measured you. People are more interested in your present and future glory than your past successes. They are always looking at what you say and do, not on what you have done or boast about. Albert Schweitzer said, "Example is leadership."

> Example is leadership Albert Schweitzer

The Past in Example Setting

There is no effective leader who hasn't come to terms with himself—knowing where he is coming from and where he is going. The past in example setting is what leads the present in other to produce an effective future.

It is in the benefit of every leader when mistakes are turned into stepping stones for success. Leaders who don't learn from their past and past mistakes keep repeating mistakes.

You see, others might not have set good examples for you, but as a leader, you cannot afford to lead without modeling or showing good leadership-act or attitude. Treating people the same negative way you were treated is a form of retrogressive leadership. As Zig Ziglar stated, "It's not what happens to you that determines how far you will go in life; it is how you handle what happens to you."

Setting an example

In parenting, children imitate what they see their parents do. So it is when it comes to leadership. Followers adapt to the ways (ethics and values) of their leader. You are the seed of the fruit your organization produce. Meaning, you are the inventor of what behavior is demonstrated in the organization. Whatever behavior followers or employees depict can be said to be the acceptable norm of the leader. That is why coaches and managers are held *responsible* in sports for a team's failure. Why? Because the performance of the players depict a picture of the leader's influence.

It is the same reason why leaders are blamed when an organization fails or the reason why presidents are accused for bad governance. It is also the reason why parents are generally blamed for the misconducts or bad behaviors of their children. Because the principles a leader sets are what his people follow and what followers do (consciously or unconsciously) is seen as the satisfactory standard of a leader. As a result, everything rises and falls on leadership.

You must realize that the activities in your organization are representative of what you value. You are responsible for every behavior your people demonstrate at work. Whatever you model, followers follow through with you. The practices around you can be said to be the characters you accept; for who you are is who you attract. And who you attract is not determine by what you want. It's determined by who you are."[7]

In setting up an example use…

1. Occurrence

Good examples can be derived from the past; it is the best reason why you must know how to handle offenses. When a leader doesn't learn anything from occurrences, then his leadership becomes sentimental. And leadership has little to do with your thoughts and feelings. Leadership deals with reality—what is right. If your paradigm (viewpoint) is wrong, you will act erroneously, if it is right (principle based) you will act truly; for It is according to a leader's view he acts.

> Leaders are the shortcut to their organization and followers' breakthrough

Your leadership will be judged by the effect you have on it. True Leadership is a shift in paradigm—in a different way of thinking. Most of the great leaders we know are not those who had good things happening to them. I don't come from a worthy or elite family or community but my life has become a model for others.

Successful leaders set examples not necessarily because they had it modeled for them. It's just that they see things differently and act realistically. They don't behave badly towards others because that was the way they were behaved towards. Although they were not shown respect or trusted, they prove it to others. Some set examples by loving and encouraging, when no one loved and encouragement them. Author Sam Cawthorn pointed out, "The happiest people don't necessarily have the best of everything but they make the most of everything."

True leaders produce good acts from bad ones. They make the best out of every life's situation. You don't need good things to happen to you before you set good example. All you need to do is to embrace principles in order to act realistically.

2. Yourself

In setting example, a leader must know, he is the example; not his position. Don't be a leader who says to his people *"do as I say and not as I do"*, leaving your *leadership-acts* in dualism. When a leader thinks words are everything he places value on them. But won't you agree to it that what we do communicates more of us than what we say?

In example setting, words become valueless if it doesn't drive action. It is like the inscription on a cigarette park which says, *"Smoking can be harmful to your health."* The inscription has lost its value because the harmful product never ceases from production. It is the categorical reason why many leaders are losing trust today. What they point out for people to avoid is what they end up embracing. So to set an example, you must become the example yourself—not by expecting it from others.

3. Attitude/Behavior

Many leaders think they are not supposed to model any imitated behavior; they think people must model themselves. But when a leader doesn't depict good morals for himself and the organization, his bad habits loses him trust and respect.

When a leader doesn't exhibit good morals, the unexpected always happens because there are no guidelines for people to follow. As children bring outside behaviors home when there is no home model, so will employees or followers satisfy their ego in an organization that has no introduction for any acceptable behavior.

When you set good morals in your organization, you uplift the morale of people; build credibility for yourself and the organization. The examples you set reveals to others how things are expected to be. A good leadership example helps followers to understand leadership models.

As I have observed, leaders are the shortcuts to their organizations and followers' breakthrough. So lead consciously. Example setting should be one of the topmost priorities in your leadership life because it is what measures leadership. As author Huston Smith asserted, "The most powerful moral influence is example."

Example key

The number one key to influencing others when it comes to example setting is to build *TRUST*. Followers will not go along with you because you are *trying* to set an example; they will because you are an example.

Trust is built; it is not given nor gotten. As simple as it sounds, when people don't trust you, they will not draw close to you, and if they can't pull themselves towards you, they will not follow you. And note: if they can't follow you, they will not accept you as a leader, and if they can't accept you as a leader, they leave you to stand alone. That's when you look back and realize although you have followers there is no one following.

Develop Trust

To develop trust, a leader must be...

1. **Truthful**: *Do what you say and say what you do—your words must equal your action.* Don't talk positive and act negative. You don't agree with people and oppose behind their backs. You don't call for a meeting and never show up. You don't make promises and refute it. You don't hide the truth and speak lies.

   Followers or employees will be truthful to you, your clients and each other if you exhibit that quality around them. People do what they see.

2. **Respectful**: *You receive in return what you give.* What really goes round also comes around in leadership. The way you treat people will determine the way they will treat each other.

   In building trust and respecting others, you must treat people the way they *should be* treated. Goethe taught, "Treat a man as he is and he will remain as he is. Treat a man as he can and should be, and he will become as he can and should be."[8] Not only if you respect your people will they respect you, in return they will respect each other. People practice what people see.

3. **Understanding**: *When followers don't understand you, they will not follow your leadership.* Don't be a convoluted leader who takes what's simple and makes it complex in other to feel bossy as the school system have taught us. Become a bottom-line leader; a person who is able to take complex issues, breaks it down into simple form so a common view is shared. And your people will also learn to embrace such practice when they are communicating to each other. People imitate what they see.

4. **A Servant**: *Understanding goes with service.* In leadership, examples are not easily set. It comes through great sacrifice. As a parent, you set example because "of" (your children, or to build a reputation). As a manager or leader, you set examples because "of" (credibility: for yourself and for the organization). So, leadership examples are set because "of". Every leader has his own reasons why he sets example. You must find and embrace an appropriate one. When you serve your people, they will learn to serve each other, the organization and its customers in return. Instead of becoming positionally-minded or salary-oriented.

5. **Team-player**: *One person sets an example while others make up for its measure.* The feedback or response you receive in your organization determines the type of example you are setting. If you don't show love, care and affection towards your people, no one will force himself to build that culture.

   Followers easily imitate what they see in their leader. And If you want people to work cooperatively, create a work relation—an atmosphere where people can work together to produce a common result despite differences.

IN SETTING EXAMPLES

You must know that examples are set and followed—they are not set to expect. To set an example, you must demonstrate trustworthiness and the fruits of trustworthiness are….

TRUTH
RESPECT
UNDERSTANDING
SERVANTSHIP
TEAM PLAYING

Remember; People do what people see. Learn to model the behavior you want followed.

CHAPTER: 7

ATTITUDE

Weakness of attitude becomes weakness of character.

— Albert Einstein

We have heard oftentimes that attitude is everything. And yes, attitude can be said to be everything because it is the difference maker; it is what makes or breaks a person. While we are certainly not our attitude, it is what represents who we truly are. The way you feel, think and act are the results of your attitude.

Attitude is derived from experiences—our personal encounter with the world. It is experience that molds and reveals attitude. The way we all feel, think and act, are the outcome of our experience. That is why I don't mostly blame people because of the way they make public their attitude. As said, the environment in which a man grows up can determine his behavior. So also with our attitude; for we were not born with it, circumstances and situations determined it for us.

A different world

One of the reasons why many leaders don't become effective is because of their emotions—they have allowed it to influence their attitude. They think they are their sentiments. They carry their feelings and use it wherever they go. And when you ask them, "why are you too emotional dependent or why can't you excuse your feelings on issues?" They will remark, "This is who I am", "I was born this way." But the truth is, it's not who they are neither what they were born with. But rather the way they were brought up, how people dealt with them and the way they saw the world and predicted things to be based on their encounter, experiences and understanding of the world.

Leadership is a shift in paradigm. What situations have made you cannot be taken into leadership if you want to model and become a successful leader.

When a leader's sentiments (feelings) go ahead of him, it destroys his *leadership-competence (the ability to do what is right)*, because his emotional baggage begins to pull his leadership abilities back. But when a leader considers his attitude as a difference maker, feedback becomes an important tool towards his leadership growth.

A sense of knowing

Attitude originally gives value to who we are and it brings out the best in us. Every man needs attitude to depict his character. Without attitude, character cannot be activated. Our feelings and thoughts are what align our nature. The human nature will be disorganized without the act of feeling. But as good as feelings are, if not controlled will destroy many of the things it comes into contact with.

The only difference between successful and unsuccessful leaders is very simple; successful leaders have discovered who they are and led themselves. And the only thing that triggers discovery is action, and action comes from acknowledgement—the ability to make real a thing.

Attitude Product

Ineffective leaders fail to lead because they promote more of their sentiments in leadership. They put what they feel ahead of their character, competence and responsibilities. And because it's their feeling that dictates their leadership, they make and change decisions carelessly. Their words don't correspond with their deeds. What they feel is what they do. If they feel to lead they lead by dominance—signaling they are in charge

However effective leadership is not what you think, neither what you feel nor say—it's about whom you are and the difference you can make. Your thoughts and feelings are for you—*they are supposed to judge your leadership-act* or attitude. As a result, your judged action must depict your attitude. Before you try to change someone or a behavior in an organization, change yourself first, for you cannot force *change* on people but you can model change for them.

A true leader understands that the moment he changes everything around him adjust to such change. Successful leaders don't demand change, they expect it; *meaning, they don't wait for people to change before they do—they change and expect followership.*

Followers don't change and expect their leader to follow rather it is the leader who changes and expects followership from his people. The type of attitude you depict is measured by the kind of leader you are. And your attitude as a leader will determine the type of people you attract, not by who you are.

Leadership Thought

Attitude is an act—a settled way of communication. Your attitude should be personal—it should reveal your behavior, not to fight others. A leader who doesn't work on his emotions will hurt others with it.

When a leader's attitude becomes his sentiments (thought and feeling), he begins to think he was made a leader because…

There was no wiser person found other than him,
He is smarter than his colleagues,
He knows better than others,
He is the right man for the job,
He is more special,
He attended the best school,
He comes from a notable family,
He has the best contacts or connections,
He is a good communicator.

His ego never seizes. And such a leader will indispensably amount to nothing than an opportunist and a competitor. You are not made a leader because of what quality you *think* qualified you. You are made a leader because a responsible person was needed to establish or carry a particular course on.

The Leadership Attitude

Even though we are the governors of our attitude, we don't reward it. When you depict good morals in your organization, it makes people to recognize your leadership and label it as a true one. Many people are struggling in leadership because they have placed position above character, thinking position is what gets things done.

To become an effective leader, your *leadership-act* or attitude must lead and incite people to produce needed results.

Attitude

One notable disadvantage about attitude is that it does change irrespective of priority. All of us can attest to things we used to cherish that doesn't interest us anymore. One of the desires of a student is to learn hard, obtain good grades, so he can get a safe and a secured job. As a result, they set their priorities right by revolving their attitude and activities around the things that matter most. And when that dream comes alive, you will find them cruising in life because they have hit their mark in life.

> You cannot force change on people but you can model change for them

Ineffective managers and leaders are like these graduates. They aspire to be leaders and the moment they become, they place themselves in a comfortable position—a place where they can fold their arms, put their feet on the table, and start playing sentimental game of feelings. What they feel is what they do; as a result, their *leadership-act* is based on feelings. They are leaders who say and do the opposite—their leadership-act cannot be seen any closer to what they say. Whiles their people cannot tell what type of leaders they are serving, they the leaders don't see anything wrong with their leading.

Maintain Attitude

Feelings come and go, ideas come and go, thoughts come and go, authority comes and go, and so can you lose focus as a leader. Every man has the ability to change his personality (what he has become) but none of us can change who we truly are. So the fact that you are depicting good morals today doesn't mean you will end well—you must maintain a positive attitude in other to finish well.

That is why it is very important for you to know when to act on feelings and when not to. When a desire or feeling is expressed wrongly, its effect becomes damaging. That is why you must note the outcome of every emotion you are displaying. An attitude that is demonstrated out of feeling is an act that pleases one man and leadership doesn't stand for an individual, it represents two or more people.

Priority

Every right attitude is set and followed; it is what establishes priority. When a communicator's main concern is towards effective communication, it becomes number one on his priority list. And for most of us, anything we want to do, have or achieve becomes our priority—isn't it? Likewise with a true leadership attitude, it must be *set* and followed. When you want to be an example, you must set it by paying attention to your deeds.

Priority is a principle that organizes interest. Every leader has interest—things he regards and pays critical attention to. For some, it is their feelings and thoughts that become their leading picture. And if it is your feelings and thoughts that dictate your attitude, your leadership becomes personal, rather than task and people oriented. Even though leadership is much of self, it's better a service—it must serve people.

When a leader becomes too personal in leadership, he tends to focus on himself and "*careless*" about anything. However, true leadership is different; it is putting principles ahead of self.

Each one of us has feelings and thoughts. The way you manage yours will determine how successful you will become. James Allen stated, "You are today where your thought have brought you and you will be tomorrow where it take you."[1]

True leaders are those who work on their thoughts and feelings—they learn to manage them. What you feel and think is not what you should exercise, because every thought and feeling must be examined with facts and true leadership requires that. Feelings must be examined to make sure they are not drawn from self or ego but it conforms to true principles. When feelings are drawn from self, it satisfies one man, when they are based on principles, it pleases everyone else. For example, when an employee does a mistake, effective leaders' don't first react; they investigate the cause of the mistake and deal with their people based on such findings and not on their immediate thoughts and feelings.

Effective leaders are those who understand issues before reacting, whiles ineffective leaders react to matters before getting to understand. It is what differentiates attitude from personality (self). Attitude puts principle ahead of personality while personality puts self before principle.

When you place yourself (feelings and thoughts) ahead of principle, assault will be inevitable because your *leadership-act* or attitude will be based on sentiments and not principle centered. But when you place principles above personality, lessons are learnt and future mistakes are prevented.

Have you ever acted in a way to someone and later realized you acted unreasonably? Whereby you were unable to hold up so as to know *'the what'* or *'the why'*, but you only acted based on your immediate thoughts or feelings. How did you feel about your uncontrollable emotion afterwards? It hurts, isn't it? That's what an act without facts produces—regret. The way you handle your thoughts and feelings will determine the type of leader you are.

Thoughts and feelings are what make and break leaders. You must understand the consequences of an act before exhibiting it. Never place your feelings above principles rather place principles above your feelings so that your *leadership-act* will correspond with your response.

Your thoughts and feelings must rightly direct your acts. A leadership-act that is not judged and controlled destroys reputation. When a leader places his feelings before facts, people are abused and neglected but when principles come first, people sense good judgment, feel appreciated and loved no matter the chastisement.

> Whatever you blame also has something to blame-and nobody gets better at last

Attitude towards work

At least all of us want to be known and to have influence in certain areas of our lives. But not all of us get involved in what we anticipate. Many are interested in the leadership position but are not ready to give up what's required for it. Most of us want to become leaders because we are conversant with the managing and commanding aspect but true leadership goes beyond power display.

When a leader doesn't get involved in his leadership, not only will mistakes compound, trust will also be lost. You cannot sit behind your desk and expect work to be done, you must be involved. The old traditional leadership of *"I'm the boss"* has become relic. Don't just sit behind your desk, pass on work, put your feet on the desk and yell for results. Results don't produce themselves—it takes effort, and you must participate in achieving them. You must be available to provide guidance and direction where and when necessary.

Don't be a leader whose interest lies in getting results and rewards. Telling people *what* you want without providing *how* will not mark you as a true leader. Your attitude towards work will determine how followers regard you and will value work. As Winston Churchill observed, "Attitude is a little thing that makes a big difference."

Involvement

Effective leaders are those who drive their team to its desired destination. When managers sit behind while *"employee's-assistance" (support and help)* is needed, mistakes abound because there is no supervision. Followers don't know *how* to do *what* they are expected to, until they are taught and left to do it. And it's your responsibility to provide guidance.

Effective leaders have an open room for further discussions and directions. Don't be a leader who is unavailable when *employee-assistance* is needed. Never delegate without letting your people know they can call or come to you when they need help. And when you delegate, know that you are *responsible (accountable)* for the outcome, not your people.

Leaders who blame employees are those who don't accept their responsibility and such a leader cannot be said to have a good attitude. True *leadership-act* involves the acceptance of blame; it is the reason why not all managers like delegating, because they will rather do it perfectly themselves than to delegate in uncertainness. But when an effective leader delegates he assumes full responsibility.

|| Attitude is an act ||

Attitude as an Act

Attitude is an act because it embodies the way we think, feel and respond to instances. Majority of leaders have abused their *leadership-act.* They have allowed their thoughts and feelings to dominate and influence their leadership. As a result, they are leading egoistically because they cannot excuse their emotions.

When there is no priority—a set standard—in leadership, we abuse our influence and neglect the people we are leading. Although attitude is an act, it is not to prove your positional authority but to manage your behavior. When your feelings are to judge your actions, your leadership-act will be exhibited consciously. The reason why some leaders regret their actions before realizing them is because they place feelings above issues—instead of excusing it.

When a leader excuses himself from feelings, he releases himself of anger, thereby acting reasonably over a mistake. But when a leader's act is based on feelings, he loses *focus* and ends up hurting people. Former U.S president Dwight D. Eisenhower observed, "You don't lead by hitting people over the head - that's assault, not leadership."[2]

Judged Actions

Every action of a leader must be judged before taken. When you judge your actions before they are made public, you act reasonably. And this act of reasonability is what makes people to recognise your leadership and to label it a good one.

True leaders don't act *"On"* when an employee makes a mistake, rather they act *"By"* — meaning your reaction or attitude on a cause of an employee or a followers' mistake is not to hold blame but to question the cause (the reason) of the mistake so as to prevent it from reoccurring in the near future.

When a leader act *"On"* when there is a mistake, his focus diverts from what can be done to prevent it from reoccurring in the future, to who did *what* and how he can hold that person accountable for the mistake. But note, you can never get or grow bigger than the things you blame. What ineffective leaders refuse to comprehend is that who you blame also has something to blame. If you blame your people for a mistake, believe me, they will also find something or someone to blame. Because if everything was well planned, all will have gone according to plan.

But when a leader acts "*By*" he acknowledges a mistake has been made, however his focus is not on '*whom*' but rather what measures can be enacted to prevent such mistake(s) from happening in the near future. After all, that is why you are made a leader; to help solve problems. I'm not saying, as a leader you are not supposed to get angry but what I mean is this; exercise your anger wisely—not to satisfy self, but for the benefit of the organization and its people.

I remember when I was working with my former boss George Koomson at Price Ghana Ltd. When we make a mistake, fear grips our hearts because we don't know what his reactions will be. As much as we try to predict what the outcome will be, he always surprise us when he realizes what had happen. His actions are not immediate as we think. I can tell it hurts him when we make mistakes but he always exhibits great *leadership-act*—by putting principle ahead of self and ego. Then after he has deliberated and calmed himself down, he calls us and asks:

"What happened, why did you move out of routine? You have just wasted money, you know very well, you shouldn't have done it that way" —now that is principle (putting first things first). "When it happens again, I will deduct two percent out of your paycheck" —that is emotion. Then his last words, "what can we do", —that is solution seeking, the way forward.

The story is told of Thomas J. Watson Snr, the founder of IBM who called his senior vice president to his office after the vice president has just lost ten million dollars of the company's money developing a new product line that had failed. The vice president came into Watson's office and said immediately, "I know you are going to fire me for losing all of that money, I just want you to know that I am sorry and I will leave without causing any more problems." Watson replied with these words, "Fire you, you must be kidding, I have just invested ten million dollars in your education. Now let's talk about your next assignment."

> People don't leave their company, they leave their leader
> -John Maxwell

Such a boss is a leader who puts principles above self (feelings). Although feelings are there it has not been prioritized but laid aside. When you think before acting, your *leadership-act* and judgments become accepted, directional and big picture oriented. In the last tycoon novel, Francis Scott Fitzgerald observe, "Action is character." Or let me simply put; "action defines leadership."

Egoistic

The reason why some managers don't succeed in their leadership role is because they think they can do everything with position. Their ego communicates to them…

– oh, you can do it,
– you are the leader,

– just say it and it will happen,

– what are you waiting for,

– Start the process; they are waiting for your command,

– This position is what you sacrificed for, it's what you spent years working towards—don't allow anyone to steal it from you.

And once these thoughts start running through a leaders mind, fear starts to grip him and the only way he can break out of such fear is to prove to his ego, "yes I am in charge and no one can talk to me when I have not asked for their opinion". Allowing his thoughts and feelings to become his counselor—what he feels safe with. He will not like to get close to his people neither allowing them to come any closer to him. The only time he communicates to his people is when he is delegating or in need of something, but habitually he is emotionally unsociable. His leadership-act is determined by his ego.

However, true leadership doesn't relate much with self, it acts on realism. Never allow your ego to dictate your leadership or else you will not exhibit good morals.

Team building

Effective leaders are those who build teams wherever they are. The reason is that they believe in the abilities of people. Not only do they have faith in people, they also believe team building helps build good relationship that makes the work place sociable. The organization shouldn't become work-centered without concern for people. The organization should also become a place where people can share ideas and life's challenges—a place where they can seek for advice concerning their life and personal choices.

> Action defines leadership

When a leader makes it known to his people that they are a team, it boosts their morale and communicates how important they are and how significantly their inputs have been. If you don't make it clear to your people you are both important, not long before they start seeing the selfishness in you. Their feelings of not been valued will compel them to emotionally disengage from you. Peter Drucker stated, "The leaders who work most effectively, it seems to me, never say 'I'. And that's not because they have trained themselves not to say 'I'. They don't think 'I'. They think 'we'; they think 'team'. They understand their job is to make the team function. They accept responsibility and don't sidestep it, but 'we' gets the credit….this is what creates trust, what enables you to get the task done."[3] You see, if employees don't get along with their managers, don't like them nor respect them, they will leave a company despite a high salary or great benefits.[4]

Feedbacks

Effectiveness doesn't fight for itself, it must be reached. The fact that you are effective today doesn't necessarily mean you will remain successful. I have observed leaders who were once successful but have been forgotten and those who were unsuccessful that have raised the standard for themselves, all because of their daily response to circumstances.

You must be careful of the things you involve yourself in. Your attitude is what defines you; you can choose to give it out (lose it) or you can choose to keep it (improve on it). It is always true that we don't naturally change; our attitude is what does. Our thoughts change, emotions and ideas change—so can our attitude.

Attitude is mostly derived from beliefs and philosophies. So don't think your success today can stand up for tomorrow. No matter how hard the number one numerically stretches itself, it can never become two but for it to become two, three, and four and to keep progressing, it must reach out. So a good attitude today cannot promise you victory tomorrow. It is the best reason why you must always pay critical attention to your communication and dealings with people if you want to remain effective as a leader. I always feel sorry for leaders who don't like receiving feedback.

Feedback is the only thing that communicates the true performance of a leader. And if you don't like what you see, you can change it. Author and poet Maya Angelou pointed out, "If you don't like something, change it. If you can't change it, change your attitude. Don't complain."[5] Most at times, we don't know where we are and how we are doing until we are informed or come to that point of realization. I have come across leaders who make their wives or children their feedback agents. They remark, "Honey, if you see or notice any bad behavior from me, please let me know."

Change doesn't happen naturally; for it's a choice, it must be embraced. Probably the reason why some leaders don't change their wrong behaviors is because no one makes it known to them or probably those who get informed never see anything wrong with their behaviors. If you hate feedback, your ego becomes your adviser. And if it's your ego that dictate your leadership, I can guarantee you one thing; *you will become a leader who is full of himself without respect, attitude and character.*

Feedbacks as Change

The reality about feedbacks is that it doesn't lie, it only points out our true self. Most feedbacks might not encourage you when you realize or receive them; because it doesn't seem to represent who you perceive yourself to be. But note this; leaders who don't accept reality, end up embracing idealism.

Feedback is like a portrait, it reveals who you are—in or at a particular point in time. I guess it would have been difficult for any of us to believe each other of how his or her face really looks like without the help of any

> If you don't like a thing, change it; if you can't change it, change your attitude
> -Maya Angelou

reflective object. However, reflective objects like mirror only reveal what's placed before it. That's also true with feedback; it depicts how you are leading. And if you don't like what you see, the good news is, you can change it.

As a leader, you will not be able to notice all your leadership flaws, some will be presented to you, and it will take courage to accept, consider and make amends if needed. When you say *no* to feedback, remember, you are unconsciously saying *yes* to ego. And that pride can ruin your reputation and make you lose credibility.

Feedback is one of the essential tools towards leadership growth. One of the attributes that can indicate whether you are growing as a leader is how you respond to feedback. Feedback puts you in a position; it notifies and informs you of a current act. And when employees or followers present you with feedback, don't send them back with it—accept it, analyze and judge it with facts before making amends. Read books and attend seminars in that direction and if a change is needed, submit yourself to such change.

Thoughts and Feelings

Thoughts and feelings produce excellent results when they are exercised appropriately. It's our feelings and thoughts that inform us of what may happen but it can't guarantee that. That is why as a leader, your thoughts and feelings must always be premised on facts, truth and realism. If your feelings and thoughts are influenced by facts, your *leadership-act* will be recognized as a good one.

Our emotions are meant to make us but unfortunately our inability to harness them causes them to break us. How you exercise your thoughts and feelings will determine how it benefits you, the people and the organization you lead.

Cultivating a Good ATTITUDE

In cultivating a good attitude;

1. Do what you say and say what you do.
2. Don't base your leadership-act on feelings and thoughts.
3. Judge your actions before making it public.
4. Accept feedbacks and work towards progress.

Remember: Your attitude represents who you are.

CHAPTER: 8

DEVELOPMENT

"The task of leadership is not to put greatness into humanity, but to elicit it, for the greatness is already there."

— John Buchan

Almost every leader I have met in a leadership position wants to be known as a great leader. They want to leave a legacy in the minds and hearts of the people they lead. Many never realize they are not leading until they are no more in power. It is what saddens the heart of some former presidents; they only ask themselves the *leadership question* of whether they were leading, when they are out of power. When they are in power, they never take the time to ask themselves what type of leaders they are. The kind of reputation they are building and whether their personality favors their relationships. They are very busy for what they can achieve for themselves and their country. And not the type of people or parents they are, and what they can do for the people who represent the country they lead.

While they are in office they think they are satisfying needs, and as they step down; they get to realize they were only pushing for personal interest. Other fortunate presidents also realize it in their last term of office; they have not done what is needed and important so they fight to maintain power in order to live a good name.

Unfortunately, some leaders take the shortcut approach, by bribing followers (trying to promote them or open doors of opportunity for them) when their term of office is expiring, because they want someone to speak well of their leadership. Others as I know want to uplift their leadership and people but just don't know the steps to take. Some never try at all but want to be recognized as a great leader.

One of the disadvantages I have seen in leadership is that it can become political—power struggle. And when leadership becomes that it turns into competition; a *win-lose* game, whereby

I *(the leader)* wins and you (the employee or follower) loses. However, effective leadership doesn't take sides; because leadership is the ability to persuade someone or particularly people to *willingly* do what you want. As a result, both win. Truly effective leaders don't only look at what they can make happen for themselves or their organizations but also what they can do for the people they lead.

Leadership and Politics

When leadership tends to politics instead of responsibility minded, managers feel threatened by the potential and capabilities of their people. So they use power to subdue their best people in order to protect their turf.

Every true leader teaches his people and gives them an opportunity to do what he does. He even becomes happy when they do it better than he teaches them. Dictating to people is good, it feels good but it will not mark you as a great leader—sharing power is what does. Co-founder and chairman of Microsoft Bill Gates stated, "As we look ahead into the next century, leaders will be those who empower others."

Core Values

In leadership, followers adapt to the style of the leader. In fact the attitude employees or followers depict is said to be the *set* standard of a leader. Although people will adapt to you, they can also distinguish between right and wrong, even if they've allowed themselves to be led wrongly.

You are the person who determines how things are in the organization. Don't be deceived that because you have followers, you are leading. People can follow and not call you a leader. Just because you are the boss doesn't mean you are a leader—you can be followed and be disliked.

If your leadership principles are wrong so is your *leadership-act*, for we only act based on our core values. And if all you place values on as a leader is work, activity and self—guess what, you will keep people in boxes, but if you value people, you will add value to them.

Leadership responsibility

Once you become a leader, you should understand; leadership is full of responsibility. It has nothing to do with relaxation. As I've observed, many people aspire for the leadership position and the moment they achieve it, they settle—with the assumption that they have arrived. But you must realize that leadership is a place where activity begins, not a place where it ends.

When a true leader gets into leadership, he first positions himself because he understands, everything rises and falls on him—*the leader*. When a leader thinks the position he occupies is to make him feel safe, he tends to use it in other to protect his turf. As Myles Munroe commented, "If you find your value in title, you are in trouble."[1]

Realize that your position as a leader is not to make you feel superior over others. It is to get things done. And never protect your position because you want to feel safe, share power because you want it to be used to get things done.

Leadership expectations

In a sense, it seems followers know more than their leaders do. In every organization, employees expect more from their managers than their managers know or give. If we take parenting for example, children expect more from their parents than their parents think they have given or provided. It is said that children (infants) naturally think their parents are rich, although it doesn't really seem so for all parents. But that is their assumption of the world they live in. And it is this mindset that encourages them to continuously make demands and even to ask for the impossible sometimes.

> If you find your value in title, you are in trouble
> —Myles Monroe

When it comes to leadership, such childish acts can be seen. Employees are always expecting from their leaders and if you're an observant leader, you can identify with that. But the truth is; you cannot meet all the needs of your people by just providing for them. Provision is good, it answers a request but it doesn't put demands off. Managers who struggle with employees' relationship are those who try to meet every avoidable demand from their people but true leaders don't chart that course.

Effective leaders train and teach people how to handle their own wants and needs. When a leader doesn't teach his people to become responsible on their own, they think they are the leader's responsibility—so they leave their lives in his hands.

It's a human instinct which states; if I can't blame myself for self-failure then someone else must take the blame. And guess who is culpable for their failure—*you, the leader*. Why? Because you've become their responsibility.

When children don't become response-able at certain age (say 30 or 40), they become a burden to their parents, isn't it. The same applies to leadership, when you refuse to teach your people to become responsible on their own, they will continue to think their livelihoods depend on you. And when you become fed up with their unmet emotional needs, they label you selfish.

Leadership development

Leadership development comes by sharing power with people. Leaders who hold power (depend on it) don't lift up others. Leadership development is necessary and essential. As a leader, you need to realize that you cannot succeed alone. And even if you do, your success will either have little or no influence on others.

Development of people is what makes every leader to achieve true success. Success is not about achieving personal goals or self-satisfactory results; true success is in adding value to people. Author and formal CEO of General Electric Jack Welch write, "Before you are a leader, success is all about growing yourself. When you become a leader success is all about growing others."[2] Every true leader helps others to become better than they are.

To develop others, you must:

1. Sacrifice for them

Author Ken Kesey stated, "You don't lead by pointing and telling people some place to go. You lead by going to that place and making a case."[3] Leaders who take others where they want them to be are those who have been or are there themselves; because you cannot give what you do not have.

Leaders who lift up others are those who have taken the high road—they are developing themselves. They are leaders who are turning mistakes into experiences. They are not only positional occupants, they are responsibility minded.

If you are in the process of nurturing others, you must offer them what works—not what you have tried and failed at. Growth is not motivation. When you want to help people grow, teach them principles. Never use people to test a theory you failed at, recommend to them what makes one succeed. What you have not practiced, don't merely teach. Give out what you know works and it will be worth their efforts. Don't put people on trial and error expedition.

When I was in high school, there was this amateur teacher who used us his students to learn what he was expected to teach. Whatever he studied and did not understand, he brought it to class for the best students to solve and to provide him with the answers. The ones we were unable to solve got him angry, frustrated and sometimes made him to leave the classroom or make it homework. This happened for some time and one day, some students reported him to administration on a homework which didn't make sense but he had insisted on it to be solved. And when he was asked by other math teachers to solve the equation, he was found wanting.

When we struggle through the airport and finally get into the airplane we're not the ones to worry about flying. We leave that responsibility in the hands of the pilot; for it is his responsibility to take us from where we are to where we must get to.

Education; effective leaders take people on a journey they are on, not the ones they want them to embark on. It will be very difficult to take people on a journey you have no direction to. There is one quality I've discovered about people who influence us. We allow them because they connect our hearts and minds to what they are associating us with. And, it's in that view and assurance that we are persuaded to follow what they are relating with us. Successful leaders also possess such characteristics, and it's what convinces their people to follow them. You can best take people as far where you've been.

Don't be a leader who tries to use assumptions and information to uplift people. As my friend Michael Paa Kwesi Asare said, "Motivation doesn't last, it is for a moment. The only thing that takes a person far is education, what they've learned." I have observed leaders who use information; that is, what they have read or heard to inspire their people, thinking it's what shapes a person. Motivation is only for a moment but education is what teaches and instructs a person through the course of life—it is what inspires self-motivation. Telling people what they can do is good, leading them through it, makes a difference. Don't only be interested in what employees do for the organization, be concerned about what they can also do, that will add value to their lives. Remember, you are the shortcut to your follower's breakthrough.

The reason why our school system has failed is because it only teaches, it doesn't lead. But successful leaders teach and lead—and that's your *"servant-ship"* responsibility (service to man). James Donald Walters asserted, "Leadership is an opportunity to serve. It is not a trumpet call to self-importance"

2. Encourage them

One of the hindrances to some leaders when it comes to uplifting others is the lack of courage; they have no faith themselves. It is the underlining reason why a leader cannot give what he does not have. It is also what sets apart leaders from teachers. *Leaders lead while teachers teach.* Effective leaders don't go on strike because their people refute to follow their counsel. They don't give up on their people because they fail to pass a test. Neither do they demand the impossible from them; rather, they lift the pressure off their shoulders. Successful leaders don't lead because they *have to*; they lead because they *want to*—it is a course commitment.

Teachers move with their feelings, leaders give up their feelings. A teacher *thinks and feels* it is the student's responsibility to understand what he teaches, but a leader *knows* it is his responsibility to make his people to understand what he teaches. It is the core reason why leadership goes beyond titles and position.

The process; Just because you want others to become independent doesn't mean they will love to follow you. It is not everyone who wants to become self-governing. But as a leader, you must help your people see the benefits of becoming independent. It is easy to motivate people to do what they are being paid for but very difficult to encourage them outside their commitments. Every employee has his or her own challenges in life. And they have no choice than to pretend they are okay coming to work; for they think nobody will understand them when they share their private affairs or probably it may interfere with work. But when a leader goes beyond just job description and takes into account the well-being of his people, it helps and uplifts their morale.

Although some employees have the spirit of sharing, not all do. And, a leader is not to wait for his people to approach him before he knows what's happening in their life; a true leader takes that initiative. It is the reason why leadership cannot be based on feelings. You don't have to wait to feel before getting to know the people you lead. If feelings are imperative to you, then the wellbeing of your people will never be known or matter to you.

> Effective leaders take people on a journey they are on, not the ones they want them to embark on

If a manager's response to his employees is premised on his status or feelings, his employees do what they do without any improvement. Your people are what they are to you because of the way you see and treat them. But when you move out of your comfort zone to help encourage them, work done becomes effective and accurate—as a result, everyone wins. John Maxwell asserted,

"When you develop others, they become better, they do the job better, and both you and the organization benefit. Everybody wins. The result? You become the kind of leader that others seek out and want to follow because of the way you add value to people."[4] Isn't that true. When a leader helps his people, in return, they help him and the organization—as a result everybody wins.

Listening; United States Secretary, David Dean Rust observed, "One of the best ways to persuade others is with your ears—by listening to them."[5] Employees only open up to managers and leaders who are ready to listen and to give counsel based on what has been discussed. In encouraging people, many leaders do the mistake of pushing in what they want to say, thereby neglecting the concern of the converser. When that happens, the converser feels he or she is not been listened to.

In listening, you must do so with intent. You must be ready to listen to the converser's heartfelt, regrets, frustrations, bitterness and perceptions. Not until the converser sees this interest in you, he will end the conversation—after all; it's his concern, not yours.

Then after you've listened, you must share in his feelings and hurts. And when providing solution, let it be in harmony with what's been discussed, or the converser will think you were not listening so why must he listen to you.

Just imagine I'm your boss. You come to me and state, "An employee is getting you angry by using a fault you committed in the organization against you. And I respond, "If you did not do that mistake will anyone use it against you?" How will you feel about such a response? But assume I say, "All of us in this organization have made one mistake or the other and that is no big deal. So stop listening to that pretender and focus on your work. Although you made a mistake, we have all learn from it. As a company, we use mistakes as a stepping stone for success. And your mistake have shown us how things don't work. Never mind that, just keep doing what you've been employed to do." How will you feel after that? You see, it's not what we say to people that hurts but *how* we say it is what makes all the difference. To touch the soul of another human being is to walk on holy grounds.[6]

Ability: When encouraging followers, do so based on their strengths, gifts and talents, not on their weaknesses. For there are no benefits in our weakness, the value can be found in our ability—what we've been empowered to do.

3. Believe in them

Faith is the antidote for growth. When uplifting people, you need to exercise faith in them. Writer and Evangelist, Hal Lindsay noted, "Man can live about forty days without food, about three days without water, about eight minutes without air….but only for one second without hope."[7] There is a seed of faith in every man, and not until it is watered, success will be far away from him. When a person has faith in himself he can do unprecedented things. But when there is no faith, failure then exist. Everyone who has succeeded did so because they believed they could. There is no one who has ever succeeded without the existence of faith; for faith is what makes possible.

I wouldn't have been where I'm today if significant people like, Joshua Abbey and Bright Ladzekpo did not have faith in me. It was Joshua—a minister of God at the International Central Gospel Church—who first saw and believed I could come this far while I was yet a teenager, and that investment in me is what has brought me this far. Bright—former manager, Altar Media—was second; he gave me an office and placed me behind a sophisticated gadget and a desk when I knew absolutely nothing about a computer. And those basic things I learnt are what have made me a computer literate today. All because someone believed in me.

When we believe in people, they do better than we even expect of them. As a leader, you must learn to incite hope and to encourage your people to achieve great results. Napoleon Bonaparte affirmed, "A leader is a dealer in hope."[8]

4. Value them

Until people know how important they are, they will not convince themselves. Until a person knows what he has, he cannot make a difference with it. When a person doesn't know the value of GH¢100, he can set it on fire.

Many people have neglected their ability because they believe they cannot succeed like others have. That is why in uplifting people, you must reveal to them how important they are and how capable they can be. Use examples to make them realize the value of their efforts, time and talent and how significant it can be if they build on it.

Encourage them to attend seminars in their area of strengths (talent) and recommend other materials (like books) for them. I've seen leaders who practice favoritism with their people when it comes to development. Don't compare someone with another—only use verifiable examples to encourage. And don't treat them the same; delight in them according to their talent and ability, not on their weaknesses. When you begin comparing people, division comes into existence and hatred compounds. Love them for who they are, praise them for what they have and have done, reward them for their achievements and persuade them to become excellent. Maya Angelou commented, "I've learned that people will forget what you said…what you did, but people will never forget how you made them feel."

5. Give Them Credit

In the workplace, every employee wants to *feel* important. It is an emotional salary every employee wants to be paid. When organizations don't show the important aspects of their people, it signals to them they are not that important. This is also true in leadership, when employees feel they are not important to the leader, they find ways to withdraw from him. Although some may not leave physically, their emotions will be long gone.

In uplifting the morale of your people, you must let them know how important they are to you—by letting them know how significantly their inputs have help you and the organization. Some leaders do the mistake of thinking their people must need them. They play the political game of win-lose.

If you make yourself too important and inaccessible, you import impossibilities into your leadership. Industrialist Andrew Carnegie said, "No man will ever make a great leader who wants to do it all by himself or to get all the credits for doing it." Every leader is important to his people as well as his people are also valuable to him. No one should be belittled. One of my observations as a leader is that *people can succeed with or without you*. So why not credit them for their efforts. It's a leader's commendation that builds faith, hope and trust in followers.

6. Challenge them

People like challenge, in fact they need it. Employees become jaded if they find themselves doing the same thing over and over again. Challenge is what makes work very enjoyable and loved. Some leaders I know, delegate not necessarily because they want to give out work, but because they want to see the efficiency in their people. Every follower enjoys it when their routine changes or becomes challenging.

Successful leaders challenge their people by delegating part of their responsibilities to them. Others also do so by assigning different tasks to their people. I know pastors who delegate their preaching responsibilities to their assistant pastors. There are also managers who delegate a day or a week's assignment to an employee or allow them to represent him at a meeting. I've come across teachers who give their students a chance to teach on a particular topic.

When you constantly challenge your people, it helps them build momentum, learn, unlearn and relearn; as a result, they develop certain leadership abilities that aid them to perform better. When you challenge people, it helps them to expand their circle of influence.

7. Reward them on every level

Reward is an emotional salary every employee wants to receive from his boss.

Reflecting back, I remember when I started working with Joshua Abbey. I can't say I got everything right or I did everything as it was expected of me. Although some of my efforts caused work delay, I can't also say it was not recognised and appreciated.

Although some of your people may not be performing at a level you want, you still need to appreciate their efforts and to let them know how they are performing. Letting a person know how he is doing on a task or assignment is a form of appreciation and encouragement. It signals and communicates to an employee you are observing and realizing his efforts.

Negatively, I've met managers who offend their employees instead of rewarding them emotionally. And when this happens, it's not only the employee who suffers, the organization and the leader also does. Dismissing people will not mark you as an effective leader, it rather makes you worse; as other employees are observing your leadership attitude. Although you may not like the progress of an employee, encouragement and education is what will challenge him towards improvement.

> A leader is a dealer in hope
> -Napoleon Bonaparte

8. Help them revitalize

Every employee or follower has a goal in life. The fact that people are working doesn't mean they are fulfilling their objectives. Work is just a means, never think you are doing an employee a favor because you are paying or determining his salary. Salary doesn't motivate employees; it is fulfillment they are after. If you want to know whether this saying is true, just take time and ask your people what their sincere goals in life are. And it will surprise you to know, what they really want to do, who they really want to be, the life they want to live and the type of person they want to become. Some of them had those dreams before they got employed while others design theirs on the job. But the nature of work has shut down their dreams.

When you are working with people, you must not only be interested in what they can do for you and the organization, you should also be concerned about what their dreams are—what they can do for themselves. And if you identify it, take responsibility and help them to embark on that journey. Don't be a leader who loves to keep people or followers. Be a significant leader—a person who makes the lives of others more meaningful. How would it feel, if someone should stand up in public tomorrow and say, *"if not for you"* they wouldn't have been where they are. All because you moved out of your comfort zone and lent a helping hand.

IN DEVELOPING PEOPLE

---

1. Sacrifice for them
2. Encourage them
3. Elevate them
4. Value them
5. Give them credit
6. Challenge them
7. Reward them on every level
8. Help them revitalize

Remember: True leadership is about significance—adding value to people.

EFFECTIVE COMMUNICATION

"When you communicate with others, recognize that clarity is power"

— *Stephen M.R. Covey*

In his book *'Everyone Communicates, Few Connect'*, John Maxwell writes, "Connecting is everything when it comes to communication." Even though we all communicate, only few of us connect. This is often because we don't talk to people in their language.

I personally believe 99 percent of all human confusion is centered on miscommunication. Whenever there is miscommunication, there is lack of truth and when that happens, understanding becomes difficult.

Misconception

I have interviewed managers who easily get upset because an employee doesn't get a delegated assignment well done. They seem not to understand why the error, or where the mistake is emanating from. And guess what, instead of sitting down to analyze why delegated work is not carried out properly, they tend to dismiss or blame employees. They hire new staff and realize the problem still persists. In their frustration, they assume employees are lazy, so they end up employing themselves—thus becoming a manager and an employee at the same time.

Though we all communicate, the way we want things to be seen and done most often is not meticulously how we communicate it. Assuming employees will understand what you've delegated or communicated is the greatest mistake you can ever make. Understanding doesn't come to people because you've spoken to them. David Berlo said, "Meanings are in people, not in words or symbols."[1] In the end, as John Maxwell maintained, people are persuaded not by what we say, but by what they understand.

You must understand that employees don't see things as you see them because of the differences in responsibilities. A leader's view is not the same as his people. And until you come to this realization, so as to communicate to people in a language they will understand, every delegated work will be completed in assumption.

Communication

Before I move on, let's consider communication. I am personally convinced that, all successes and failures depend on communication. In '*33 Irrevocable Laws of Wealth Creation*', Matthew Ashimolowo remarked, "Communication is the flow and exchange of life." We can make our lives, work, relationships and marriages better depending on the way we communicate. How we communicate is the "*What*" results we get.

Employees become and thrive in an organization by the way they are being communicated to. A child will turn away from an awful state because of the positive affirmations made to her. We do things because we know we can. Nothing gets done without verbal or nonverbal communication been part. So if communication is very significant in life, why is it that we don't learn to communicate effectively?

When it comes to leadership, communication is nothing short of sharing and conveying a common message. A leader cannot communicate effectively without knowing *how* to communicate. Just because you have assigned work doesn't mean it will be carried out or executed precisely. The way you want it done is the way you need to communicate it, so it's understood and done in that way.

There is no assumption when it comes to leadership communication. When you import assumptions into leadership, you create problems instead of solutions. When you don't communicate effectively to your people, they will find counsel in themselves.

What communication involves

Communication involves five things:

1. *Connecting*: Before communication, there must be a relationship. For relationship is a bond which joins two people or parties together. When there is no connection between the communicator and the receiver communication becomes thwarted.

2. *Listening and identifying*: In communication, there must be only one voice heard at a time. Henry David Thoreau maintained, "It takes two to speak the truth: one to speak, and another to hear." Many voices in communication are what create confusion and what result in misunderstanding. Two people cannot be talking at the same time

in communication and expect to reach common ground. Leaders who become effective communicators are those who pay attention to what they say and how it is being received.

3. ***Have a Cause***: In communication, there must be knowledge (information) before understanding—a point where the receiver gets to clearly see and appreciate what the communicator is communicating to him. If people cannot picture what you want, they will not grasp what you mean.

4. ***Know what you want***: Employees don't probably get work done expectedly because their bosses don't explicitly communicate what they want done. In communication, you *only* communicate what you want done—*nothing more nothing less.*

5. ***Take Action***: Probably, the greatest mistake in communication is misdirection. When you communicate, lead the way. In leading the way, you show your people the *'how to'* so it can be done in the expected way.

Leaders and Followers view

Employees don't always see from their managers or leaders point of view. In fact it is not part of their job description. And because not all employees see as their managers see, work given without clarification will be executed on assumption. General Collins Powell stated, "Great leaders are almost always great simplifiers, who can cut through argument, debate, and doubt to offer a solution everybody can understand."

In other to make your people see what you want, you must communicate 'how' you see it and want it done to them. The vision of every leader is not the lookout of followers. While followers are looking at *what* to do successfully, managers are looking on *how* what's done can satisfy needs, win customers as well as build a reputation for the organization.

In an organization for example, the employees' focus is not on how things should be done because they are not the decision makers. Their focus is on *what there is to be done* in other to keep their job and also to earn possible organizational bonuses.

Employees see where they are, leaders see where they must be. So to win with people, you must get them involved in your vision or they can't help you. It's what Stephen R. Covey stressed on that, "Involve people in a problem. Immerse them in it, so they soak it in and feel it is their problem and they tend to become an important part of the solution."[2] Until people can grasp what you are communicating, expectations will be difficult to meet.

The leaders view

A leader's responsibility is always different from his followers. And as a leader, you cannot afford to be making common mistakes. When a follower makes a mistake, it is mostly accepted but when a leader does, it has major consequences. Why? Because it is assumed, the leader must know better.

Since employees see differently and will use assumptions to get an unclassified work done, you must help them to see things from your point of view when communicating to them. And when they see as you've clearly shown them, your presence will not be needed for an expected work to be done because they already have the picture of the end in mind.

Beyond communication

True leaders go beyond communication and delegation. In every organization, employees already know *what* to do because it is their job description. So they don't need *"what to(s)"* anymore but you can always show them *"how to"*—because it's your responsibility to make sure what's done is in the best interest of the organization.

Clarifying Expectation

Anthony Robbins pointed out, "To effectively communicate, we must realize that we are all different in the way we perceive the world to be and use this understanding as our guide to our communication with others."[3] In clarifying expectation, you must make sure, the person you are communicating with, doesn't leave your presence *assuming* he had understood what you've said but you must ensure he can communicate precisely what you've said to another if he's expected to delegate that assignment for another.

In clarifying expectations, a leader must…

1. Build Work Relation

The reason why many mangers face scrutiny, pressure and disappointment is because of lack of building relationships.[4] Relationships are very vital in leadership and work ethics. When a leader refuses to connect with his people, his people also refuse making any effort towards him.

Relationship is an emotional connection—a bond which joins two or more people together. You don't connect with employees because you want to; you connect because you *have* to. It is a two way affair.

Relationship is not one time event, it's a process. It is not something that happens once, it is an association you stay and get along with. You don't get to a point in a relationship where you say, "*Ah*, I've related so let me move on with other things." Relationship is a daily activity—an association you stay or get closer to always. Employees will not continue to respect you because you are the boss, they will because you have built a relationship with them.

Don't be a leader whose focus is to just get work done; be a leader who builds a relationship that meets expectations. Your people will understand you quickly and easily if they have a relationship with you.

When people are connected to you, they can more or less tell where a conversation will end before it even gets there. Relationship brings out and creates a picture of a leader's ethics and values in the minds of the people he relates with. It is not easy for followers to understand a leader, until they know him. And how do we know people—through relationships. When people are close to you, they become familiar with your leadership principles (your yes and no) and because they have those values in mind, it becomes easy for them to understand you in communication.

> Don't be a leader whose focus is to just get work done, become a leader who builds relationship that meets expectations

Effective relationship is what gets things done in an expected way. Have you ever worked with a boss who you hardly look in the face when he or she is talking to you? You cannot look him in the eye comfortably and confidently agree or disagree with what he is saying. That is a good sign of a weak relationship and it doesn't generally get desired things done. If you have to yell or shout at people before they listen to you, then you better observe your attitude and relationship with people. Remember the words of Dwight David Eisenhower, "You don't lead by hitting people over the head–that's assault, not leadership." Don't turn the workplace into a busy activity firm; let it become a related place for work where understanding and simplicity is a norm.

To build a relationship with people, you must:

1. **Respect them for who they are**: Everyone has his own way of visualizing things and you should not disregard that as a leader. Just because followers don't see as you see, doesn't mean they cannot think or make good decisions. Human right activist Malcolm X said, "Don't be in a hurry to condemn because he doesn't…think as you think." If you look down on people, you cannot build a relationship with them. Love them for who they are.

2. **Be a friend**: Just because you are the boss doesn't mean you are more important than anyone else. Friendship is not a sign of weakness as many leaders wrongly believe; friendship is actually a sign of strength.

   I've worked with different kinds of leaders for ten years. Some got work done expectedly, others fought me over it. But as I look back, I realize those who won with me, were those who had a relationship with me. Relationship is what engages the heart and mind of people through commonness.

3. ***Reach Common Ground***. Stephen M. R. Covey writes, "When you communicate with others recognize that clarity is power."[5] Ninety nine percent of human confusion as I alluded to is the cause of miscommunication. As a result, every failure or success depends on communication. Work is successfully done through effective communication.

> When we pressurize people, they bring the pressure back to us

When you communicate effectively, you get ahead, when you don't, confusion and apportioning of blame is what takes over.

   Common ground speaks to the all-important issue of understanding. And understanding in this context refers to a leader's ability to make complex things simple.

   The fact that you communicate doesn't mean it will be understood at that level; for people don't see as you see. What may seem simple for you might be complex to the receiver. So when you communicate, you should understand that it's not in your interest but in the favor of the person you are communicating with because he is the one going to carry-out what you've said to its completion zone.

Until the receiver can grasp what you are communicating, you only leave him to assumption and almost nothing is achieved. That is why in communication, you must make sure the heart and mind of the receiver is engaged to see, understand and agree to what you are transmitting. Everyone likes clarity. Even people who are not bottom-line thinkers want to know the bottom line.[6] When you *assume* you are making sense when actually you aren't, confusion is what you leave people with.

In reaching common ground, you should be able to give meaning to what you are communicating. Many leaders think communication is only delegation—so they pass on work and wait for result. But leaders who reach common grounds are those who go beyond just talking, they establish agreement through *discussion, repetition and feedback.*

Discussion: When it comes to work discussion, some managers tend to argue with their people. They always want to put their point(s) across. They don't care how employees get work done, all they are interested in is that 'It should be done well.' They threaten and intimidate employees with work. But from what I have seen, people don't work effectively under pressure. When we pressurize people, they bring the pressure back to us. That is why effective leaders make time with their employees to talk, so their people *understand* what they are c-o-m-m-u-n-i-c-a-t-i-n-g. That is, having time for a personal heart-to-heart talk about what you want done. True leaders don't communicate or delegate in a hurry because when a leader rushes in communication, he distorts facts.

> The first time you say something, it's heard. The second time, it's recognized and the third time, it's learned
> -William H. Rastetter

Repetition and feedback: William H. Rastetter observed, "The first time you say something, it's heard. The second time, it's recognized and the third time, it's learned." In communication, we mean what we are communicating by how meticulously we communicate it. I know your people are not deaf but there are followers or employees who listen in haste. And if you don't exercise patience so you can connect their heart and minds to what you are communicating, they will find counsel in themselves and because they don't see as you see, guess what, assumption is what will lead them to get confused work done.

Therefore if you communicate, I encourage you to make sure you have been understood, not heard. Don't be satisfied when the receiver responds, "I hear you sir or ma'am." Make sure their hearts and minds are connected to the message. If possible let them communicate it back to you and if it needs to be repeated—repeat it the second, the third or the fourth time for understanding to be establish. Les Landes wrote, "Don't ask people if they understand what you mean, if you want to make sure they understand something important ask them to repeat what you've said until you're satisfied you share the same meaning."[7]

2. Identifying Your People

In clarifying expectations, you must know the temperament of your people. Not all employees possess the same spirit when it comes to understanding. I have observed three human spirits when it comes to understanding task.

The *first* category of people understands things the moment they see it; these types of people are *leaders* themselves—they are easy to work with. They understand work once it is communicated.

The *second* group of people, I call *managers*. These are people who need things to be communicated to at their level of understanding. These people are a bit difficult to work with. Although they may see things from your point of view, they asked themselves, "Can I do it?" These are people who need encouragement and support. Letting them know you are there for any assistance makes them feel rest–assured.

The *third* kinds of people are very skeptical. I call them *lay-hold*s. These classes of people are not easy to work with. They like doing routines. They don't like change because they think they cannot handle it. They are the type of people who will need critical attention from you *the leader* to get any task done. They are always asking for direction and guidance. They ask questions like "what next?", "what do you think?", "am I doing well?", and "is it ok?"

As interesting as it may seem, positional leaders like working with the third group of people, because it always make them feel important and needed. And as difficult as it may sound, effective leaders do their best to work with all three groups of people, because knowing whom you are communicating to, is what gets communicated.

3. Say It As You Want It

Shelley Lazarus observed, "The people I have problem dealing with… are people who tend to not give full information…they distort facts."[8] In clarifying expectations, you must only communicate what you want done—*nothing more nothing less*. When you are communicating; communicate work, not self. When followers don't understand what should be done, they get nothing done or get it done through assumption. So when you communicate, recognize that clarity is power.

4. Make provision

There are leaders who want things done without thinking *how* possible. In communication, whatever must be done need to be possible; possible in the sense that whatever provision is needed to get a delegated work done is available. A teacher cannot set an exam question for his students on subjects they have not been taught and expect them to excel at it. That is why before possibility, there must be availability. You must let your people know they can count or call on you for any assistance. Don't just pass on work; let employees know there is an open door for further discussion and for any additional clarification.

Clarifying Expectation

In clarifying expectation you must

– Recognize that *"How"* you communicate is *"What"* results you get

Remember: When you communicate, recognize that clarity is power.

CHAPTER: 10

REWARD

"You get what you reward. Be clear about what you want to get and systematically reward it".

— *Bob Nelson*

One of the remarkable things most of us do today in other to be recognized, accepted, be grateful to, appreciated and loved is through giving. The *act of giving* is either to get us close to people or for them to get closer to us. Don't we all love to be remembered by children, parents-in-laws, half-sisters, brothers, friends and even strangers for what we've done for them? Don't you feel honored when someone you've helped call or come to you and say thanks? In-fact these are things we considerably do for others in other to be seen, known, feel loved and cherished by them—an opportunity for us to be reminisced.

Time for Hard Talk

Although the offering of charitable acts is good as a service to mankind, they are not significant when it comes to leadership reward. A true leader doesn't reward people because he wants to be loved, cherished, connected to, or to be merely remembered. A true leader rewards because he wants *what's* rewarded to be embraced as a perfect model.

When a leader gives out reward, it signals to people of a *desired* achievement, behavior, attitude, character or model. And it's very important for you as a leader to know *what* you are rewarding because whatever *action, practice, behavior, character, achievement or attitude* you reward gets followed. Bob Nelson advised, "You get what you reward. Be clear about what you want and systematically reward it."

Isn't it true that whatever people encourage us in doing gets replicated by us because we think it's worth the praise? In leadership, reward should not be given because there is an activity. Reward must be given because a *desired* goal has been attained. Although you cannot afford to discourage the efforts of your people, you cannot also afford to ignorantly reward it. Efforts must be noticed and encouraged, not to be rewarded.

Not all activity (actions, movements or activities) gets *desired* goals achieved. John Wooden observed, "Never mistake activity for accomplishment."[1] The fact that there is an activity doesn't mean a desired goal will be attained. When you don't know what to reward and how to appreciate, then whatever action you reward gets repeated by your people.

When reward is based on activity, then I can guarantee activity will become the work focus of people. They will not risk for anything different than what gets them rewarded. And if you reward activity, activity will become the center of work for your people. However, if you reward results—producing it will become the work focus of your people.

Assume you are a manager who has assigned two groups of employed sales personnel to go out and make sales for the company's new products; let's label these two groups group A and group B. Although these two groups (group A and group B) have been going out on sales activity days, it's only group B that strives to make 40-70 percent of sales. Judging by their performance, how are you going to reward these two groups of people? Are you going to do so based on activity or based on their returns?

If you reward them the same, then you will continue to get the same produced results from them—whereby group B make sales while group A make the effort to. And because you constantly compensate group A for their acts towards sales, guess what, they will not make it a priority to sell. Why? Because intuitively they know, 'whether they make sales or not, they will get what everyone gets.' And habitually, all group A will be undertaking is to come to work, take products round, talk to people they are not willing to convince, come back to closing time and close for the next day's *"repeated"* activity.

When people don't get the desired result you want, you need to time them out; by letting them know, what they are doing and to inform them on what results they are expected to produce. Not to reward them for an activity that does not produce a *'desired'* result. Letting people know how they are doing on a job is more helpful than discouraging all or what they've done.

When activities are rewarded, it signals results are no more important. It's one of the ignorant mistakes some leaders and managers make. That is why in leadership, you cannot *assume* to be doing things right, you must get the right things done.

Looking Back

I entered into the job market when I was seventeen years. And in my ten years of working with leaders, I have observed many *leadership-acts*. The first leader I worked with knew how to reward results and to acknowledge efforts. I never understood why all of us worked towards results but at the end, only few get rewarded. Although he was not that effective, he understood the principle of return—what gets rewarded, gets done.

Then in 2003, I worked with another leader. To be honest, he is responsible for who I am today. He understood the leadership principles and exhibited them meticulously. As I started working for him, I noticed two things; reward and recognition. Although not all of us get desired results, he didn't discourage those of us who made the effort towards achieving them; he affirmed, "You can do better, keep on." And because of his affirmations we were also able to achieve great results.

Right and Wrong

As a leader, you must know what to reward and how to appreciate. Right things must always be done right. When right becomes right it forms a principle but when wrong is made right it breaks a system.

How to Reward Results

In rewarding, you should focus on *what's* rewarded, not *who*. We don't reward people— we only reward the results they've produced. Appearance can be judged but evidence cannot lie. If we are all rewarded for efforts (activity) towards a particular course at work, I don't think any of us will ever aim at getting results, because it will not challenge us.

> You don't reward people- you reward the results they've produced

When you reward your people for activity, their chances of working towards results will be very minimal. Employees are not looking up to you the leader to have mercy on them because they know it's the worst form of practice you should avoid. Employees hold in high esteem when a leader is honest with them. Although you might be ignorant of it, they regard it.

Virtually, every employee knows how each worker performs in an organization, even if the leader doesn't inform them—they can assess it. That is why employees will find it very difficult to become emotionally engage with a leader who fakes reward.

When a leader begins to play favoritism when it comes to reward, he breaks trust and loses competent people. The worst thing that can happen to any leader is when he is being surrounded by sycophants (yes men).

When given out reward, you must be honest; for it is in honesty that *trustworthiness* is produce. And the fruits of trustworthiness are *truth, respect, understanding, sincerity and sharing.*

Truth: When employees realize you are not realistic with them, they will not *willingly* follow your leadership; for no one gets along with a leader who cannot be relied upon. William Clement Stone observed, "Truth will always be truth, regardless of lack of misunderstanding, disbelief and ignorance"

Respect: People like to be around like-minded men. When your people get to know you have no respect for them, in return, they disapprove of your leadership and show you no respect.

Understanding: If you don't know how to distinguish feelings from realism, your *leadership-act* will be premised on emotions, which will lead you towards bad leadership.

Sincerity and Sharing: Everyone likes to know the truth. Even a thief who's been caught, wants to know whether the accusations laid on him can really prove whether he stole what he is been accused of stealing. Genuineness is what everyone is looking out for in a leader. If people cannot see sincerity in you, they will emotionally disengage from you.

Even those who don't deserve reward know you are cheating on someone when rewards are given in favoritism. First of all, reward has nothing to do with a person but the results produce.

What is Reward?

When we talk of reward, most people look on appreciation. Yes it might but emphasis is not laid on it when it comes to leadership. Leadership reward goes beyond human acts or services. As I alluded to, people give reward out of appreciation or for appreciation; to say thank you or to establish a relationship. However, in leadership, you give reward because you want *influence* from what's rewarded. You don't give because it will help you remain in power, to be accepted or to be loved—that practice breaks trust.

The law of reward states that what's rewarded must have a reason for why it is rewarded. In an organization as I indicated, almost everyone knows how each worker performs. So in that context, reward should not be faked. Critics don't get annoyed when reward is given; they get angry when it's given without a reason. Every reward must be accompanied by its cause *(the reason why it's rewarded)*.

Three steps to consider when rewarding

1. What is to be rewarded or "The what" of the reward?

What is rewarded can either be an attitude, behavior or a result produced. If you're rewarding a person, the reward must go for *what* he either stood for or *what* he has done. Not who the person is, because who is rewarded is not as important as *what's* rewarded. Result is what observers or accusers (those who are not rewarded) will be looking at. Accusers or employees are not looking at the person who is being rewarded; their focus is on *what's* rewarded. Results are what matters to accusers. If you are rewarding *who* then I suggest, everyone should be rewarded.

2. The impact of the reward

The effect of what's rewarded is also as important as the reward. The transformation of what is rewarded must be noticed. Not until accusers can see the impact of what's rewarded, they will disapprove of your leadership. You must show the influence or growth of what you are rewarding because those who are not rewarded want to be convinced.

3. The fact of the reward

Every reward must produce something. And, the produce of such reward is its evidence. Until accusers have something they can use to judge the reward, they will disagree with it. So when you are giving out reward, make sure its evidence is visible.

If these three principles can be evident in your leadership reward, then critics or accusers will find no fault in the person or what's rewarded. Remember, everyone likes clarity.

What happens in reward?

There are consequences that accompanies a reward, and as a leader, you must be acquainted with it. True leaders don't reward because they want to, they do so because it brings transformation. Leaders, who don't reward their people, limit their leadership and organization's growth. And those who cut corners with it lose trust and respect. Who is rewarded is as important as what's rewarded. And who a reward is given to, is also as important as who gives it.

When a leader gives out a reward, two things happen. First there is *identification* and second there is *acknowledgment*. Identification represents what you the *giver of the reward* stands for, and acknowledgement signifies what you *the giver* values and expects. John Maxwell noted, "Who you are is who you attract. (And) who you attract is not determined by what you want. It's determined by who you are."

> Knowing people is the best answer you can give people.

The following procedures can also be used when giving out reward. Reward is not only a method for compensation; reward is also a form of spiritual growth and encouragement.

1. **Who An Employee Is**. Every effective leader appreciates his people. It's the antidote that gets things done precisely by employees. When a manager appreciates who his employees are, it makes them feel valued by the manager. That is why as a leader, you cannot afford to discourage the efforts of people. It doesn't matter the many errors of employees, great managers don't seize to correct, to show respect and to encourage. Elizabeth Harrison asserted, "The people who are lifting the world onward and upward are those who encourage more than they criticize."

When you don't encourage your people, unconsciously you discourage them. True leaders don't always admire every act of their people but they accept, teach, correct and work with them. I have worked with leaders who cannot accept mistakes; all they are interested in is results, results, results. They yell for results as if results produce themselves. Its people who make it happen and when you lift up the morale of people, it gets them to do what they do even better. Knowing people is the best answer you can give people.

2. **Will**. Every employee works best in his/her strength zone. Not all people get things done on the same level. When a task is given to two or more people, someone will definitely finish last, and that shouldn't become the base score for giving out reward. I know some leaders count on that. But if your leadership reward is based on who finishes an assignment first then when a task is given, people will not be cautious of how to get results. The only thing they will be interested in is how to finish first, because you have compelled them to compete with each other.

Excellence is not achieved through competition; it's attained through correct principles. When a leader's aim is to just get results, he gets it and loses it quickly because right principles were not followed.

In the market place, consumers are not looking for accomplishment but quality. So it doesn't matter how slowly or fast a company produces its products, it must be worth the purchase. It's also true when it comes to leadership; it's not how fast people get results but what measures produce those results.

If you are the kind of a leader who pushes only for results, then you will mistakenly reward fast. Fast results should be rewarded only when it follows right procedure. I don't think you will be happy if your people break organizational rules to get results. Never discourage the resilience of your people, encourage it and they will get better.

3. **Attitude**. The attitude of every employee should be considerably important to you. True leaders don't only reward accomplishments, they also reward behaviors. Leaders who only promote employees because they can get things done, end up disappointing themselves. Effective leaders don't promote people because they can handle work; they do so because they can *work with* people.

When you're promoting an employee or making a follower a head of a department or group, you must look out for the attitude of that person. In regard to:

How he sees himself and regards others,
The way he communicates with people,
And the way he or she expresses his thoughts and feelings.

If you don't look out for these traits in the person you are promoting, then that person will take his narcissism into that position, thinking he was promoted because he is the best person for that position, or he is the only intelligent one to fit in. And this self-centeredness can devastate the ability of every one under him. So when promoting a person lookout for the attitude that can positively influence the people under him.

4. **Development**. True leaders enjoy working with people who love growth. It's always the dream of every teacher for his students to become excellent in his subject. But there is one weakness I've discovered in the lives of some leaders; although they want their people to grow and become effective, they don't want them to outstrip them. This is not with effective leaders, they develop and like employees who work towards personal growth.

Don't fight your people when they are growing spiritually or mentally, encourage and reward their growth and sooner other employees will embrace such act.

Employees don't grow in organizations where growth is never encouraged. I've been there and I have seen it all. Whatever gets rewarded whether consciously or unconsciously, gets followed.

If you encourage growth, you will experience breakthroughs in your organization,
If you encourage criticism—you will be surrounded by critics,
If you encourage lie—you will work with liars,
And if you encourage hypocrites—you will be surrounded by pretenders.
Whatever a leader encourages multiplies—don't forget that.

Consequences of Reward

Every reward comes up with its own consequences. There is always a message a reward sends and it all boils down to what's rewarded. You cannot afford to reward carelessly; for whatever action, practice, character, behavior and attitude you reward, gets followed. If you reward wrong behaviors, it will be accepted by other employees and demonstrated before you; if you reward good ones, it will be exhibited before you.

What I have observed is that employees are always in the lookout for what their leader wants. And what he gives attention to is what keeps reoccurring around him. So you better observe what you reward. Every employee wants to please you as a leader, so whatever they can find or do to make them feel appreciated by you will be looked out for and shown.

> Whatever a leader encourages multiplies—don't forget that

Reward victories

Reward can send good or bad note depending on *what's* rewarded. Reward can make you to either win with people or lose with them.

If employees don't like the criteria you use to determine reward, two things happen; the potential people find their way out of the organization while the coward ones stay and fight for personal gains. They—the coward ones—will hate you for who you are, where you are and where you are heading towards. They will think no good of you or the organization and desire nothing better along your way. While you are working towards the big picture they are focusing on themselves—meaning while you are aiming at progress, they will be concentrating on personal gains. They will do everything to secure a permanent position in the organization so they can stay and work till their strengths fail them.

Playing the reward game ignorantly and carelessly has hurt many leaders and will continue to be detrimental, as long as it's practice inappropriately.

Employees Interest

Every employee has an interest in his or her organization and that interest is to do things in the best interest and notice of the organization. That is why they will demand fairness. Employees don't get angry because you find out they have done something wrong, they will because you found out and never led them in the right direction. John Wooden observed, "A coach is someone who can give correction without causing resentment."

Have you ever heard this words from your people, *"I thought"*, *"I assumed"*, those "I" with hypothesis. Whenever you hear this, note, people are not clear on what they are doing and your leading will be very helpful. Reassigning tasks to other employees will leave incapable ones in resentment. And because you don't give them any other task apart from what they routinely do, promotion will be far away from them and their longevity in the organization can cause them to blame and hate you for where they are.

Letting people know what their setbacks are and what they can do to stave them in other to earn organizational benefits will help them aim at it. Never be ashamed to recommend personal development programs for employees who need it. Because when they develop themselves, they help you and the organization. As a result, everybody wins.

REWARDING

In giving out reward, you must…..

1. Realize that rewards are not gifts neither are they for recognition.
2. Apply '**the what**', '**the Impact**' and '**the Fact**' of the reward principle.
3. Only reward what you want done or followed.

Remember: Whatever gets rewarded gets done.

How to Lead Like a Leader

To lead like a leader, you need to;

1. Develop a learning attitude in other to become a committed learner.
2. Model the behavior you want followed.
3. Renew your attitude—personality.
4. Grow your people.
5. Learn to communicate effectively.
6. Reward expectancies.

It seemed difficult to become the best at all six. But what I know is this; you can become better than the six if you make them a skill in your leadership and managerial position.

Part 3

MAKING WISDOM
APPLICABLE

CHAPTER: 11

LEGACY

A good man leaves an inheritance to his children's children

— Proverbs 13:22 (NKJV)

A good name is to be chosen rather than great riches, loving favor rather than silver and gold.

— Proverbs 22:1 (NKJV)

Many of us take it for granted, but leadership is one of the most difficult positions any one can occupy, or a title you should place on yourself and boast about. I have met leaders who think because they are influential, everything will respond to them auspiciously.

Effective Leadership is centered on realization (defining reality), preparation (planning) and growth (development). Leaders who don't chart the course towards effectiveness are those who end up throwing their reputations away.

Leadership has got nothing to do with titles, positions or control. When a leader sees or thinks of leadership as a destination (a place of arrival), he only seeks out for his personal interests of; what to have, the clothes to wear, the cars to drive, the food to eat, the people to be associated with and the kind of mansion to live in. But when a leader takes his eyes off self, he sees and act differently. The scripture made it clear that, "We should *love* our neighbor as ourselves."[1]

Loving your neighbor as yourself is a leadership responsibility God bestows on us—to take into account the wellbeing of others as we do of ourselves. The golden rule states, "Do unto others as you would have them do unto you"—or as I put it, "do to others as you will *expectedly* want done to you."

Has it not become a norm today to reject the poor and admire the rich? The world has created a misconception for us. A myth that says, you cannot afford to be at the bottom—not even to serve others. So ignorantly, nations are competing against each other to prove to themselves who the best is. As a result, we (husbands, wives, children, families, friends or colleagues) are also competing against each other. How easily have you seen the rich accommodating the poor— just because they (*the rich*) have a *false* belief which states, "Rich people don't associate with the poor; we are looking for people of class." Even so, the poor are also fighting against one another, sacrificing to build a relationship with the rich, leaving the like–minded, noble and teachable people behind.

But I see love in a different way. When the subject of love comes up I see *language, obedience, value and encouragement.*

1. Language. Love is a language that must be learnt. People don't understand us in communication until we speak to them in their language. South Africa Formal President, Nelson Mandela pointed out, "When you talk to a man in a language he understands, that goes to his head, if you talk to him in his language that goes to his heart."[2]

There is a language every man best understands, and it takes patience and concern to establish that connection. Talking to people is a formal way of conversation but going beyond your understanding to theirs is what empathetically builds common ground. You cannot understand a person until you know how he or she thinks.

2. Obedience. Mainly, many leaders never see anything wrong with disrespecting others. They argue about it when the topic is discussed. They think their people will be losers without them. But effective leadership is centered on reciprocity—whatever a man sows that shall he reap.

If you disrespect others, they will also disregard you. Never expect people to respect you if you don't show them respect. We are all equal, and every man deserves a living being's acknowledgement.

3. Value. I've come across leaders who never see anyone as important as they are. They pull others down so they can climb up. They think they are the best thing that has happen on earth. They value themselves more importantly than anyone else. They use the weaknesses of others against them and use their positional authority to weaken any competitive strength.

However, true leadership is in the act of giving hope to the hopeless, experiences to the non-experience—in other to make the lives of others seem more meaningful. As the Chinese proverb said, "There is a great man who makes every man feel small. But the real great man is the man who makes every man feels great." Leaders who leave a memorable legacy are the ones who add value to others.

4. Encouragement. Nearly all of us think getting close to certain people will diminish and make us look vulnerable so we disconnect ourselves and don't relate with our so called 'certain people', neither do we make new friends. Just because we have been stuck ignorantly in, "birds of the same feather flock together."[3] But becoming a friend of someone doesn't necessarily mean you are a friend to him. Getting close to know, to help and share what you have and know with others is a form of support and upliftment.

Victor Hugo said, "The supreme happiness of life is the conviction that we are loved." You cannot clearly say you love a person until you:

Understand them—*their way of thinking so to know them,*
Respect them—*not because of what they are but because of whom they are (human being),*
Value them—*because you believe in them,*
Encourage them—to offer help and support.

Comfort Zone

When I meet leaders who have settled, I recommend they move out of their comfort zones before they become a barrier to their organization's breakthrough. I don't think any of us would like to be labeled *"bad"* when our names are mentioned. But believe it or not, your life here on earth will be summed up one day. And if you are supposed to write your own autobiography before you die, how would you love it to be read? Maurice Chevalier stated, "A comfortable old age is the reward of a well-spent youth. Instead of it bringing sad and melancholy prospects of decay, it would give us hopes of eternal youth in a better world."

Surface of Legacy

I believe the common meaning that comes to mind when we hear of legacy is inheritance. The MS Dictionary defines legacy as, "Something handed down by a predecessor." When you watch a relay race, you will realize that one person doesn't run it entirely. But can you pause to picture what would happen if one person decides to compete for the race. Not

> The problem you helped solve is the solution you have provided

only will he be acting selfishly, he would most likely fail. But when there is a release of the baton, the game becomes effective.

You will also observe that in the relay race not everyone runs at the same pace. Some run fast while others less but the interesting thing is, together they all win. One person's strength sharpens the other person's weakness.

This is also true when it comes to human life; most of us think we can do everything by ourselves. Although some do and do well, nobody remembers them and their achievements doesn't leave long after they are gone. However, when a leader passes on the baton; that is, when he invests his life in others and helps develop them, he leaves them with a sense of purpose. Therefore, whoever hands down leadership principles to you, determines the level of your leadership and to whom you hand yours down to will determine that person's level of effectiveness.

If legacy is an inheritance—something handed down by a predecessor—then what type of inheritance are you leaving behind; as a leader, a parent, a business associate or a friend? Walter Lippmann stated, "The final test of a leader is that he leaves behind him in others, the conviction and the will to carry on."[4] Is your life and leadership influencing and encouraging others to follow correct principle in other to do what is right or it is sidetracking them?

Paradigm shift

It is the dream of every man to be appreciated and remembered while alive and after he is dead. But why is it that we don't meet this expectation, or why is it that people are remembered and honored while alive and become history after they are gone—whereby nobody talks about them, and even those who are remembered, are reminisced just for some few months? Is it because human beings are ungrateful or is that the way of life? This is a question many of us have not sat down to ask ourselves. We leave life to chance, expecting things to work out for us. But as I cited in the prologue, *Life is not managed, life is led.* When we don't lead our lives we become optimistic of the future and care-less about the present. Men who leave memorable legacies are those who decide to do so.

> Legacy is a course for remembrance

Many of us only know how to plan towards activities, but fail to consider our destinies. When you begin to look into the future in other to plan towards leaving a legacy, your whole paradigm changes; you begin to see and understand things differently. Life becomes real; you learn to appreciate life and people more than things (valuables).

The saddest picture I have seen is that majority of people don't get to realize realism until they are in their fifties, sixties and seventies, when much harm has already been done. Whereby money has been misused, character neglected and attitude mishandled. By then, the past only becomes a wish. It is the primary reason why some presidents fight for another term in office, just to make things right (focus on reality) before they step down.

A choice

When planning to leave a legacy, I encourage you to look into situations or for people because the problem you helped solve is the solution you've provided. And on the other-hand human beings are the inheritors of every dream we have. You cannot solve the entire world's problems neither can you achieve every dream you have alone. It's the reason why, team building must be imperative to you as a person. Without people dreams cannot be pursued. That is why Habakkuk stated, "Write the vision and make it plain on tablet, that he may run who reads it."[5]

When we take our country for instance, isn't it true that our laws were written over decades ago but they are still been observed and will continue to be? Although these law inscribers are no more in power, their realistic paradigm for Ghana is still on course. All because they think generationally—and because they think generationally, they are solving today's and tomorrow's seeming problems with a written constitution.

I want you to take a break here in other to ask yourself this question, *"What of me will still be breathing while I am no more?"* If you can picture a thing, work towards it, if you can't, start planning. Legacy is not just left, legacy is planned for; it is a decision you make towards your relevance on earth. You plan for it and work towards it.

A legacy

There are many ways to leave a legacy. Legacy is not only handed down in physical forms (like money or building) as many of us think and work towards. Legacy as I will define it; *is a course for remembrance*. Whenever there is a legacy, there is a past; a commemoration. If you cannot be remembered for anything of importance, then you are doing nothing of significant value.

When a true leader wants to leave a legacy, he looks for what he can do that will *add value* to others. I guess you don't think much of people who buy you gifts than those who made life happen for you—people you can say, "had it not been for this person, I wouldn't be where I am". The way you don't brag about people who present you with perishable items is the same way others will not remember you for anything you've done that did not add value to their lives.

Ownership

Leadership legacy is a form of ownership and ownership comes with responsibility. You cannot own something that you are not responsible for. What you are not responsible for, you do not own.

However, it's very interesting people's aspirations of ownership today. I have observe leaders who want to become owners but don't want the responsibility that comes with it. Maybe in life you can fight your way through but when it comes to leaving a memorable legacy, you must take responsibility for what you want to be remembered for.

Parents, who are not responsible for their children's welfare, become nothing of significant value to their children. If a teacher is not responsible for his or her students' educational performance, then they will remember him for nothing. If a manager doesn't care about his people, their progress in life will reflect nothing of him.

Followers or employees should remember you for something of a significant value you've done for them. A person's life and success should reflect your sacrifice on it. A good name as the scripture observed is better than precious ointment.[6] We must not be the ones indebted to the world after we are gone, the world must be grateful for our existence in it. Gordon Parks said, "It's a matter of giving more to this world than you take from it, so when you die, you don't owe it anything."

Becoming an Owner

There is nothing I believe we can do best for people that can substitute legacy than giving them a career and education. Legacy is left for decades, not for a day. Isn't it true that when people do things for us we only appreciate it for a moment but when they help us in doing something, we value and owe it to them?

- When you help an uneducated person get education, guess who his education and value in life reflects on.
- When you help the helpless achieve their dream, guess who their achievements in life reflects on.

- When you help the jobless person, not only to get a job but to become better at what he does, guess who his happiness in life reflects on.
- When you lead your children through the cause of life with correct principles, guess who gets the credit for their realistic life and leadership.
- Whoever you help to become better in life will forever remain grateful to you.

We don't just value important people in life, we pay homage to them. You cannot leave a memory in the mind and hearts of people, if you have nothing there that can elicit that remembrance. Many people as I have observed are waiting to be financially secured before they offer help. You don't need to be financially safe and sound in other to help others; you can do it with the little ability you have and from where you are. Leading someone through the course of life could be the greatest thing they will ever be grateful to you for when they look back.

Men and women who leave a memorable legacy are those who turn situations around—they take responsibility for other people's circumstance.

Forms of legacy

Basically, I have discovered two types of legacies we all leave. The first is Personal or Common legacy and the second is Mankind or the Servant-ship legacy.

Personal or common legacy refers to the successful plan or design of a person. It refers to an individual's personal life plan—the pleasant life one wants to live, the things he wants to achieve for himself, the reputation he want to build, the wellbeing of his family and the vision he has for the generations after him.

> Men and women who leave a memorable legacy are those who turn situations around

Mankind or Servant-ship legacy signifies what we do for others that add value and greatly benefit them. It's a thing you do willingly—a voluntary service you offer. You do it not because you want something in return but because you want your life to be a blessing to others. Albert Einstein remarked, "The world is a dangerous place to live, not because of the people who are evil, but because of the people who don't do anything about it."[7] The world would be a happy place to live, if we all think of one thing we can do that will add value and bring out the best in others before we die.

Horace Mann commented, "Doing nothing for others is the undoing of one's self. We must be purposely kind and generous, or we miss the best part of existence. The heart that goes out of itself gets large and full of joy...we do ourselves the most good doing something for others."

What type of legacy can you associate these people with?

Jesus Christ
Mahatma Gandhi
Nelson Mandela
Martin Luther King

Kwame Nkrumah
Mother Theresa
John F. Kennedy

A Good Name

A good name is to be chosen rather than great riches...Proverbs 22:1. Personal legacy personifies you because it talks about your personhood; thus the reputation you are building, your relationship with family and the dreams you have for your children and children's children.

A good name doesn't embrace any man, it is chosen. As a result, when a man loves himself, he organizes his interest and chooses his ways wisely. When he loves his family, he builds a reputation for them. And when he cares about his generation, he leaves an inheritance for them.

I have come across people who are used to, "This is my life, let me live it the way I want." Yes it's your life but you cannot live it anyhow. Many of us would have been happy in life if our predecessors left a good name behind. Wouldn't you be proud your parent's left a good name in the minds and hearts of those they knew, have met and worked with? But because of self-centeredness, some even threw their reputations away and left nothing behind than an inherited emotional debt. As a result, some of us cannot go along with the name our parents gave to us because it's full of shame, regrets and rejection.

When you are living your life, you must consciously be aware, you are representing self, family, children and generations yet unborn. When you live your life carelessly, not only will you hurt yourself but your family and generations after are going to suffer for your wrong deeds.

It will amaze you to know that particular names are not regarded in some societies, communities or towns because of the deeds of their predecessors.

What name are you leaving behind? Benjamin Disraeli stated, "On Memorial Day: The legacy of heroes is the memory of a great name and the inheritance of a great example."

Leaving a Good Name

To leave a good name, you must first understand yourself—*what* you want and *why;* because who you are, is as important as what you do and what you stand for. Friedrich Nietzsche observed, "He who has a 'why' to live can bear almost any 'how'."

Three steps to look at when considering a good name:

1. **Respect yourself**—Words are powerful, so in communication, choose your words carefully. Many people never see anything wrong when they use wrong words. They will remark, everyone does it, so what's the "big deal."

When you say something and realize it is erroneous, don't feel proud, sincerely apologize and ask for forgiveness. Feeling big to ask for forgiveness weakens relationships, detracts trust and destroys reputation. If you're not big to offend, then you are also not big to apologize. The way we present ourselves to others determines the countenance we receive.

Respecting yourself doesn't mean rating yourself above everyone else; it means accepting reality, knowing that we are all equal—you are not important than anyone, neither is anyone better than you. Love people for who they are. When you start competing with others, they analyze and disregard you. Love yourself and behave towards others as you would want them to behave towards you.

2. **Be truthful**— Broadcast journalist Edward R. Murrow stated, "To be persuasive we must be believable; to be believable we must be credible; credible we must be truthful." 'In living a truthful life, you just have to be honest with yourself. Don't see black and say its white, neither see white and claim it's blue.

You have to let things be as they are; let a lie be a lie, wrong be wrong and right be right. Don't add to facts, neither subtract from it. And if you build this emotional account in people they will hold you in high esteem, trust and celebrate you. For if you are not truthful to yourself—who then will risk believing in you?

3. **Learn to work with people**—When working for or with people don't just work for your gain; work with love, passion and appreciation. If you are a manager of an organization, work as if you own the corporation. Put in your efforts and do your best for the organization and you will be remembered for your *extra* assistance.

As a leader working with people, don't only be interested in what they do for the organization, help them to gravitate towards their goals, dreams and purpose, and when they achieve it—they will celebrate it with you. Former U.S president Abraham Lincoln declared, "In the end, it's not the years in your life that count. It's the life in your years."

A memoir

In life, we must all leave something behind to be remembered by. There must be something, you are noted for or remembered by. Someone should one day say, "IF NOT" of you. Author and poet Maya Angelou commented, "I've learned that regardless of your relationship with your parents, you'll miss them when they're gone from your life... I've learned that you shouldn't

> If you're not big to offend, then you are also not big to apologize.

go through life with a catcher's mitt on both hands; you need to be able to throw something back... I've learned that every day you should reach out and touch someone. People love a warm hug, or just a friendly pat on the back... I've learned that people will forget what you said, people will forget what you did, but people will *never* forget how you made them feel."[8]

Mother Teresa also said, "Let no one ever come to you without leaving better and happier. Be the living expression of God's kindness."

Likewise Goethe declared, "What is my life if I am no longer useful to others."

Let your life be a blessing not only to self or family but also to those around you.

Sacrificing For Remembrance

Although we take it for granted, legacy is very important on earth. We are not representatives of earth neither are we additions of it. Our responsibility is to make the earth a better place to live. Before you leave the earth, your name must be inscribed on something and your presence must be a benefit to other people. Even if you don't regard it, generations after you will.

Remember; Legacy is a cause for remembrance.

Conclusion

The leadership acronym is based on effectiveness, not position. This book is not only for people in leadership position. In fact all of us are leaders in certain areas of our lives. These principles can be applied in life, organizations, families and ministries. Learn to follow them, and people will find, follow and celebrate you. AMEN.

NOTES

CHAPTER 1

1. Stephen R. Covey, "The seven Habits of Highly Effective People."
2. Sam Cawthorn, http://www.positivelypositive.com/quotes/the-happiest-people -dont-necessarily-have-the-best-of-everything/
3. http://en.thinkexist.com/quotes/top/

CHAPTER 2

1. Andy Yawson, KICC Ghana, "Sunny FM Ghana (message on forgiveness)."
2. John Fafavi Perez, message on forgiveness of Sins "RIC Ministry Inc."
3. John Maxwell, "Winning with people."

CHAPTER 3

1. Henry David Thoreau: http://thinkexist.com/quotation/there_is_no_value_in _life_except_what_you_choose/13627.html

CHAPTER 4

1. http://www.qualitydigest.com/inside/quality-insider-article/get-your-employees-and-co-workers-do-what-you-want.html
2. Jim Ron: http://thinkexist.com/quotation/if_you_don-t_design_your_own_life_plan-chances/295557.html
3. John Maxwell, http://johnmaxwellonleadership.com/2011/01/24/how-do-i-maintain -a-teachable-attitude/

CHAPTER 5

1. Ford Model T, http://en.wikipedia.org/wiki/Ford_Model_T

2. Mark Twain, http://thinkexist.com/quotes/mark_twain/
3. Claude Bernard, http://www.brainyquote.com/quotes/authors/c/claude_bernard.html
4. John Wooden,http://www.brainyquote.com/quotes/quotes/j/johnwooden106379.html
5. https://en.wikipedia.org/wiki/Research
6. Jack Welch, From Good to Great
7. William Clement Stone, http://thinkexist.com/quotes/w._clement_stone/
8. John Maxwell, "Your Road Map for Success"
9. Thomas Edison, http://www.des.emory.edu/mfp/efficacynotgiveup.html
10. Don Shula and Ken Blanchard, "Everyone's a coach"

CHAPTER 6

1. Stephen R. Covey, "The Seven Habits of Highly Effective People"
2. Galatians 6:7 (NKJV)
3. Anthony J. D'Angelo, http://thinkexist.com/quotation/you_don-t_have_to_hold_a_position_in_order_to_be/10308.html
4. John Maxwell, "21 Irrefutable laws of leadership"
5. St. Francis of Assisi, http://thinkexist.com/quotes/st._francis_of_assisi/
6. Whitley David, quoted in John Maxwell's "21 irrefutable laws of leadership; The law of the picture)"
7. John Maxwell, "21 Irrefutable laws of leadership"
8. Johann Wolfgang von Goethe, http://thinkexist.com/quotes/johann_wolfgang_von_goethe/

CHAPTER 7

1. James Allen, http://thinkexist.com/quotes/james_allen/
2. Dwight E. Eisenhower, http://thinkexist.com/quotes/dwight_eisenhower/
3. Peter Drucker, http://sourcesofinsight.com/leadership-quotes/
4. Forbes, http://www.forbes.com/sites/reneesylvestrewilliams/2012/01/30/why-your-employees-are-leaving/
5. Maya Angelou, http://thinkexist.com/quotes/maya_angelou/

CHAPTER 8

1. Myles Munroe, On Leadership
2. Jack Welch, "Winning"
3. Ken Kesey, http://thinkexist.com/quotation/you_don-t_lead_by_pointing_and_telling_people/213209.html
4. John Maxwell, "21 Irrefutable Laws of Leadership"
5. David Dean Rust, http://www.winston-churchill-leadership.com/leadership-quote-part9.html
6. Stephen R. Covey, http://www.goodreads.com/author/quotes/1538.Stephen_R_Covey

7. Hal Lindsay, http://thinkexist.com/quotes/hal_lindsay/
8. Andrew Carnegie, http://thinkexist.com/quotes/andrew_carnegie/

CHAPTER 9

1. David Berlo, http://www.landesassociates.com/index.php?/Meanings-are-in-people.html
2. Stephen R. Covey, "Principle Centered Leadership"
3. Anthony Robbins, http://thinkexist.com/quotes/anthony_robbins/
4. John Maxwell, "21 Irrefutable Laws of Leadership."
5. Stephen M.R. Covey, "The Speed of Trust."
6. John Maxwell, "Everyone Communicates, Few Connect"
7. Les Landes, http://www.landesassociates.com/index.php?/Meanings-are-in-people.html
8. Shelley Lazarus, http://thinkexist.com/quotes/shelley_lazarus/

CHAPTER 10

1. John Wooden, http://www.gary-tomlinson.com/media/Book_Report_-_Wooden.pdf

CHAPTER 11

1. Matthew 22:39 (NKJV)
2. Nelson Mandela, http://edition.cnn.com/2008/WORLD/africa/06/24/mandela.quotes/index.html
3. http://kmcadenhead.wordpress.com/2010/02/15/birds-of-the-same-feather-flock-together/
4. Walter Lipmann, http://thinkexist.com/quotes/walter_lippmann/
5. Habakkuk 2:2 (NKJV)
6. Ecclesiastes 7:1 (NKJV)
7. Albert Einstein, http://thinkexist.com/quotes/albert_einstein/
8. Maya Angelou, http://www.goodreads.com/author/quotes/3503.Maya_Angelou